TRANSFORMING

TRANSFORMATIONAL PIANO TEACHING

Mentoring Students from All Walks of Life

Derek Kealii Polischuk

OXFORD
UNIVERSITY PRESS

OXFORD
UNIVERSITY PRESS

Oxford University Press is a department of the University of Oxford. It furthers the University's objective of excellence in research, scholarship, and education by publishing worldwide. Oxford is a registered trade mark of Oxford University Press in the UK and certain other countries.

Published in the United States of America by Oxford University Press
198 Madison Avenue, New York, NY 10016, United States of America.

© Oxford University Press 2019

All rights reserved. No part of this publication may be reproduced, stored in a retrieval system, or transmitted, in any form or by any means, without the prior permission in writing of Oxford University Press, or as expressly permitted by law, by license, or under terms agreed with the appropriate reproduction rights organization. Inquiries concerning reproduction outside the scope of the above should be sent to the Rights Department, Oxford University Press, at the address above.

You must not circulate this work in any other form and you must impose this same condition on any acquirer.

Library of Congress Cataloging-in-Publication Data
Names: Polischuk, Derek Kealii, author.
Title: Transformational piano teaching : mentoring students from all walks of life / Derek Kealii Polischuk.
Description: New York, NY : Oxford University Press, 2019. |
Includes bibliographical references and index.
Identifiers: LCCN 2018016528| ISBN 9780190664657 (hardcover : alk. paper) |
ISBN 9780190664664 (pbk. : alk. paper)
Subjects: LCSH: Piano—Instruction and study. | Mentoring. | Music—Instruction and study—Psychological aspects.
Classification: LCC MT220.P79 2019 | DDC 786.2/193071—dc23
LC record available at https://lccn.loc.gov/2018016528

1 3 5 7 9 8 6 4 2

Paperback printed by Sheridan Books, Inc., United States of America
Hardback printed by Bridgeport National Bindery, Inc., United States of America

To Karin, Veronica, and Miles, for their love, support, and understanding of Daddy's long hours at work

CONTENTS

1. The Piano Teacher as a Mentor: An Introduction — 1
2. Teaching Gifted Students — 5
   What Is Giftedness? — 6
   Gifted Students in the Piano Studio — 8
   Ability Grouping — 12
   Strategies for Working with Gifted Students — 13
   Establishing an Effective Learning Environment for Gifted Students — 15
   Creating an Effective Emotional Environment for Gifted Students — 16
   Supporting Gifted Females — 17
3. Teaching Adult Pianists — 21
   Motivation in Adult Pianists — 23
   Challenges Faced by Adult Learners — 24
   Strategies for Teaching Adult Pianists — 26
   The Benefits of Piano Study for Adults — 30
   Considering Adult Learners by Age Group — 34

CONTENTS

4. Meeting the Needs of the Recreational Student	36
A History of Recreational Music Making	37
Research into Recreational Music Making	41
Practical Ideas for Recreational Music Making	49
5. Working with Pianists with Depression	53
Recognizing Depression	54
How Common Is Depression in Children?	55
Suicide	57
What Causes Depression?	60
Effective and Appropriate Teacher Interventions	61
6. Working with Pianists with High-Functioning Autism	65
Research in Autism Instruction	66
Designing Teaching Strategies Based on Research	67
Applied Behavior Analysis and Discrete Trial Training	69
TEACCH Method	70
Wings Mentor Program	71
Scope and Sequence	72
Other Considerations for Working with Students on the Autism Spectrum	72
Centers of Research and Practice for Teaching Pianists with Autism Spectrum Disorders	74
7. Working with Pianists with Attention Deficit Hyperactivity Disorder	77
Possible Causes of ADHD	78
Symptoms of ADHD	79
Diagnosing ADHD	81
Treating ADHD	82
Teaching Students with ADHD	84

CONTENTS

8. Teaching Undergraduate Pianists	90
The Art of Teaching Undergraduates	92
Strategies for Undergraduate Lectures	96
Helping Undergraduates Develop Critical Thinking Skills	100
Opportunities for Active Learning	102
Models of Evaluation	106
Modeling Enthusiasm for Academia	108
Maintaining a Safe and Professional Relationship	110
Learner Responsibility	112
9. Mentoring Graduate Student Pianists	116
A Brief History of Graduate Education	117
The Role of Mentor	118
The Benefits of Mentoring Graduate Students	120
The Responsibilities of the Mentor	122
Best Practices for Mentors	124
Establishing a Mentoring Relationship	126
Supporting Graduate Students	128
Assistance Beyond the Degree: Lifelong Mentoring	129
Mentoring Graduate Students in a Diverse Academy	132
10. Working with International Student Pianists	135
Designing Instruction for International Students	139
Academic Integrity and the International Student	148
11. What Can We Learn from Some of History's Great Piano Teachers?	151
Carl Philipp Emanuel Bach	152
Wolfgang Amadeus Mozart	154

Carl Czerny	157
Franz Liszt	159
Josef Lhevinne	162
Rosina Lhevinne	163
Adele Marcus	164
Leon Fleisher	165
Russell Sherman	168
Technique and Music	170

12. Bringing It All Together: Your Studio as a Diverse Set of Individuals — 175
    Societal Diversity in the Piano Studio — 176
    Diverse Piano Personalities — 181
    The Diversity of Human Development — 189

13. The Motivated and Inspired Piano Teacher — 200
    Piano Teacher Training — 201
    Continuing Education for Piano Teachers — 203

Index — 215

TRANSFORMATIONAL PIANO TEACHING

Chapter 1

The Piano Teacher as a Mentor

An Introduction

I am sometimes overwhelmed by the responsibility I carry for the students in my piano studio. Without the daily perspective gained from also being a parent, I don't know if I would regularly be able to deal with the particular responsibility that this profession demands. Piano teachers are not only instructors of music but also counselors, family mediators, performance coaches, temporary parents, life coaches, and more. Because our lessons usually are taught to individuals, these roles are multiplied. This responsibility is a great blessing and the kind of mentorship that I crave in my work.

As a young pianist I studied with Krysztof Brzuza from ages eight to seventeen and with Daniel Pollack from ages seventeen to twenty-six. Both were brilliant musicians and music teachers, but their teaching resonated because they were extraordinary mentors and even father figures. My lessons in high school with Mr. Brzuza were meandering three-hour marathons spent practicing technical rudiments, rehearsing concerto movements, talking about my friends, talking about his children, talking about a life in music, talking about a life outside of music, and so on. I remember driving home at 10 p.m. not only energized about the pieces that I was preparing but inspired about life in general. There was a gentleness in his approach that allowed me to be myself. I was never ashamed of my interpretations, my opinions, or my questions. After I played something, the response, delivered in a thick Polish accent, was always, "Derek, yes. Thank you. That was v-e-e-e-r-r-y go-o-o-d, b-u-u-u-t . . . " On paper this looks like the beginning of a stinging criticism, but in person it was a gentle beginning to a helpful critique. A feeling that Krzysztof was genuinely interested in my overall development as a young man blanketed all of this. I was not merely another student he retained to supplement his income; I was, at least in my mind, his pianistic pride and joy.

My first lesson with Daniel Pollack was frightening and exhilarating. I had known Mr. Pollack from his gorgeous recordings and his fascinating interviews in the PBS documentary about the 1990 Tchaikovsky Competition, for which he was a jury member. I was wracked with nervousness as I approached Ramo Hall at the University of Southern California for the first time as a seventeen-year-old. My first lesson began with a bang, or, rather, a strike of a match, as Mr. Pollack smoked the first of what seemed like twenty-five cigarettes during just the first movement of the Mozart Sonata K. 333. As I clumsily brought the music to a halt, he said, "Go-o-o-d, good" (in a villain's voice from a *Star Wars* film). "You play well . . . has anyone ever taught you to use your wrist? . . . We need to work on this. Now. Tell me about yourself. . . . What dorm will you be staying in? Will you be going to Trojan football games? Are you Hawaiian or something?" He asked question after question. A great educator asks questions and listens. While Daniel Pollack may be famous among his students for his long and beautiful rants about any and all subjects, his sincere inquiries were what reached me. He wanted to know me as a person. This famous pianist, teacher, and connoisseur of all things Russia and piano wanted to know if I would be going to football games.

Historically, the greatest teachers of the instrument were more than instructors, they were transformative figures. Rosina Lhevinne, one of the twentieth century's most influential professors of piano and a faculty member at the Juilliard School starting in 1924, would hear students at her modest apartment in Manhattan's Upper West Side. She was frequently heard to say, "Technique is never a goal in itself. Anyone can have technique, what is important is to be yourself. And one must listen with the heart."[1]

The life of a young person, especially a teenager, is full of turmoil, doubt, self-deprecation, foolish imitation, constant evaluation of self-worth, great interpersonal triumphs, and debilitating failures. The educational life of a young person may be occupied by impersonal standardized testing, doubts and fears about future success, competition among peers, a feeling of having failed to live up to the standards set by parents or older siblings, and at best, great realizations about one's place in the world through the development of the rational mind. The private music teacher can play a critical stabilizing and edifying role in what can be a very chaotic youth. This book examines the role of mentor, a role that a successful music teacher must inhabit in order to sustain a career as an effective educator. Because each student is a distinct individual, many types of students are discussed, from high-achieving students to recreational students to those with special needs. In addition, I examine the concept of family support as an indispensable tool for sustaining a student's motivation between lessons. Finally, I discuss a teacher's own motivation and recommend a cycle of positivity and achievement as a way to keep his or her work fresh and exciting. I hope you find this work thought-provoking, enriching, and challenging, but most of all, I hope it reminds you of the reasons why you first came to love your profession.

NOTE

1. Esther Brown, "Rosina Lhevinne: Still Listening with the Heart." *People.* Accessed March 14, 2017. http://people.com/archive/rosina-lhevinne-still-listening-with-the-heart-vol-2-no-2/.

Chapter 2

Teaching Gifted Students

The concept of gifted education has undergone major changes over the course of the past thirty years. New theories about the nature of intelligence have forced our society's concept of giftedness to change and gain greater focus and effectiveness. Legitimate charges of discrimination have forced proponents of the gifted movement to ardently defend and adapt their programs. All of these discussions have led educators to examine the methods used with gifted students in an effort to open them up to a wider cross-section of pupils. It is difficult to determine whether the concept of giftedness and gifted education is at all relevant in the contemporary educational climate, in which equity and excellence for all students are understandably emphasized. The music teacher must recognize the obvious but sometimes forgotten fact that although some students may learn more quickly or may more easily grapple with challenging content, those students are not more important than others who may not be formally labeled as gifted. Students in a piano studio are simply individuals deserving of varied and thoroughly informed teaching strategies. The effective piano teacher will understand that it is critical to obtain strategies for differentiating instruction on the basis of the unique needs of the student. Therefore, the ability to teach gifted students is simply part of a toolkit of resources for meeting all of your students' unique learning needs.

WHAT IS GIFTEDNESS?

Traditionally, giftedness has been associated with a high IQ. It has been assumed that gifted students were born with unusually high intelligence and could be easily identified by their above-average school grades and success in all school subjects. Although much of this is still true and important for teachers to understand and accept, the definition of giftedness is starting to become more robust thanks to new research in cognitive science and developmental psychology. It has become clearer that there are many unique ways of being gifted, rather than a laundry list of qualities that one must posses in order to be labeled as such. Many strategies for teaching gifted students are based on a traditional definition of intelligence: the cognitive capacity that a person is born with. Recent research has begun to call this definition into question, most notably the work of intelligence theorists Robert Sternberg and Howard Gardner. Robert Sternberg has developed the *triarchic* theory of intelligence, which suggests that there are actually three distinct and measurable dimensions of intelligence.[1] In the triarchic theory, *compotential* intelligence consists of mental mechanisms for processing information, *experiential* intelligence involves the way an individual deals with new tasks or situations, and *contextual* intelligence involves the ability to adapt to, select, and shape one's environment.

Music teachers who do not formally know Howard Gardner's theory of multiple intelligences are certainly familiar with the spirit of its concepts from their years of working with a varied group of students: There are multiple ways of being "smart." Gardner has identified eight different types of intelligence: logical-mathematical, linguistic, visual-spatial, body-kinesthetic, *musical,* interpersonal, intrapersonal, and naturalistic.[2] The impact of Gardner's theory becomes clear when one compares his many categories to the traditional IQ test, which measures logical-mathematical and linguistic intelligence only. Music teachers must consider the application of Gardner's theory of multiple intelligences when working with students who are likely to fall into any of these categories of intelligence.

David Perkins has synthesized the research on theories of intelligence, grouping types of intelligence into three main strands.[3] Perkins describes *neural* intelligence as being rooted in biology and as basically a reflection of neural efficiency: Some brains are simply more physically capable of advanced thought than are others. Neural intelligence reflects the most traditional view of intelligence, similar to the IQ examination. Perkins defines *experiential* intelligence as "know-how," or the way an individual develops knowledge of specific situations and patterns. *Reflective* intelligence, for Perkins, is a knowledge of judgment strategies, or more specifically, knowing how to think and how to persist in a train of thought. Perkins suggests that all three strands of thinking combine to create overall intelligent behavior.

Joseph S. Renzulli, the director of the National Research Center on the Gifted and Talented, has developed a "three-ring" description of giftedness. In this definition, giftedness consists of *above-average ability, above-average creativity,* and *above-average task commitment* and motivation.[4] Renzulli points out that a select group of students will demonstrate these behaviors at almost all times and across activities and that other students will demonstrate them in specific activities or particular areas of interest. He goes on to suggest that the most effective approach to educating gifted students is for educators to carefully choose content, teaching, and educational opportunities according to a specific gifted student's learning needs. Rapid development in recent research shows that intelligence is multidimensional and that it can be learned. Similarly, giftedness can also be developed in a student when the curricula provided are appropriate to the student's needs.

The identification of gifted students is a far more complex endeavor than simply singling out students who receive high scores on IQ exams, or, in the case of the music studio, the students who consistently win competitions. When educators limit their identification methods to traditional measures, there are bound to be unidentified students whose needs will not be acknowledged and addressed. One of the most glaring problems that educators face in identifying gifted students is that Native American, Hispanic, and African American students are underrepresented in gifted programs while white and Asian students are overrepresented.[5] Until teachers, administrators, and parents acknowledge that students from all cultures, languages, and backgrounds can be high-ability learners, the identification of gifted students will continue to be incomplete. It is also important to remember that high-ability students may not fit the traditional picture of a good student. In order for observation to be effective in the identification of gifted students, teachers must become aware of any and all biases, assumptions, and stereotypes they may have about who can and who cannot be gifted.

GIFTED STUDENTS IN THE PIANO STUDIO

An effective music teacher understands the power in appropriately matching the level of a challenge to a student's ability. Neurological research indicates that the best learning takes place when a student's interests and abilities are matched to the right level of challenge.[6] This can present difficulties for gifted students, for whom the content and repertoire typically appropriate at a given age level are not challenging enough. Further neurological research explains why this is the case: When a curriculum is not challenging enough for a student, the brain does not release enough of the chemicals associated with learning, including dopamine, noradrenalin, serotonin.[7]

Evidence-based research about high-ability students' experiences in public school classrooms indicates that, typically, they are not being challenged at a high enough level and, as a result, their learning needs are not being met. A national study found that, at the elementary level, an average of 35 percent to 50 percent of the regular curriculum could be eliminated for gifted students.[8] The implications of this research for the private music teacher are interesting. It is important that we correctly identify gifted students in our studios and provide these students with repertoire, studies, musical tasks, and a learning pace that are well matched to their ability level. Should this not occur, we run the risk that our gifted students will lose interest in their studies or drop the study of music altogether. The concept of *music aptitude* and the measuring of this characteristic can be a helpful way to approach giftedness in the piano student. The extensive research of Edwin E. Gordon provides much of the basis for the field of music aptitude.

Edwin E. Gordon is known for his excellent books *The Psychology of Music Teaching, Learning Sequences in Music, The Nature, Description, Measurement and Evaluation of Music Aptitudes,* and *A Music Learning Theory for Newborn and Young Children.* Gordon is also the author of seven standardized music tests, including *The Musical Aptitude Profile* and *The Iowa Tests of Music Literacy.* Gordon argues that music aptitude is a product of both innate potential and early environmental experiences.[9] Gordon's writings argue that people are born with different degrees of music aptitude and that understanding these levels can help a music teacher provide appropriate and effective instruction during early childhood and beyond. Much of Gordon's concept of music aptitude stems from his research into the concept of *audiation*, that is, hearing and understanding music we have heard in our minds.[10] He advocates developing the skill of audiation in young people in much the same way as we learn to use language, in that training in audiation requires the sequential development of four music vocabularies: listening, performing, reading, and writing. When students have successfully acquired these skills, they are ready to be taught the theory of music. Gordon stresses the importance of guiding students at the earliest possible age to develop a music-listening vocabulary as a foundation for more formal music education. He argues that by the time children enter school at the age of five or six, the most important time for them to develop their music-listening vocabularies has passed. Gordon also argues that the majority of children who enter school lack the readiness to profit fully from formal music instruction. Because of the difficulties presented in such situations, Gordon recommends music aptitude testing in order to better reach students, regardless of the level of their musical potential. Information and music aptitude testing protocols are available from the Gordon Institute for Music Learning and GIA Publications.[11] Piano teachers who wish to accurately assess the music aptitude of students whom they believe exhibit giftedness in music may benefit from becoming familiar with the work of Edwin E. Gordon and may consider utilizing the testing protocols that this researcher developed in order to better tailor musical instruction to the musical aptitude of each student in their studios.

The National Research Center on the Gifted and Talented has conducted significant and enlightening research about the instruction that gifted students receive in the typical classroom. In the center's Classroom Practices Survey, researchers gathered data from a sample of seven thousand educators and found that teachers reported making only minor modifications, if any, for the gifted students in their classrooms. Teachers who *did* make adjustments usually did so by simply assigning more advanced reading materials, providing enrichment worksheets, or asking students to complete extra homework. In the center's Classroom Practices Observation Study, researchers found that in 84 percent of classroom activities, gifted students received instruction that was not distinct in any way.[12] A number of factors in a public school education might explain why teachers are finding it difficult to meet the needs of gifted learners. The basic organizing principle of schools is that students who are the same age will have the same level of ability. In addition, very few teachers have received training in how to differentiate instruction for students of various aptitudes. Fortunately, as the concept of diversity gains traction in public education, teachers are beginning to receive more frequent and more effective training in the teaching of students of all abilities and backgrounds. Despite these improvements, the tradition of a multipurpose educational delivery in which all students receive the same instruction continues to be pervasive in most schools. Applied music instruction suffers from similar restraints, in that music testing often is determined by the number of years of study or "levels" reached. Those who organize festivals or competitions and run music studios would do a great service to all music students by considering the learning differences of every student, including those who might be identified as gifted. A possible tool for addressing this issue is *ability grouping*.

ABILITY GROUPING

This practice is a divisive issue in public education. Ability grouping is different from *tracking*, which is the practice of sorting students into different classes on the basis of their grades, perceived abilities, and test scores. Ability grouping does not sort students into multiple classes but, rather, groups students within a single classroom. It may be compared, albeit imperfectly, with a piano teacher's assigning duet partners within his or her studio on the basis of their perceived giftedness by pairing gifted students with other gifted students, and so on.

Those who criticize gifted education and, specifically, tracking, claim that varied grouping is necessary in order to ensure equal opportunities for all students. Students who remain in low-level tracks are disadvantaged when it comes to developing higher-level skills and studying enriched educational content. Critics are also correct in pointing out that minority students and those from lower socioeconomic strata are overrepresented in special education and remedial classes.[13] While proponents of gifted education do not typically support tracking, they do occasionally support the concept of homogenous grouping at least some of the time as a way to meet the needs of gifted students. Supporters of homogenous grouping worry that the slower pace of a mixed group of learners will cause a gifted student to miss important opportunities to pursue advanced work. Research has shown that ability grouping has almost no effect on student achievement across all levels of learning ability. Research shows that the instructional strategies that teachers use with groups might have a greater effect on achievement than does placement.[14] In a study of schools that had been "detracked," researchers found that heterogeneous classes were the most effective when teachers used differentiated instruction, in which individualized, varied expectations, at a high level for all students, were supported by complicated assignments across the board.[15] The possibilities for private piano teachers and the flexibility of the model of private instruction are a rich ground for meeting the needs of all students, particularly gifted ones. Research has shown that problem-solving and inquiry tasks are most effective when delivered in a heterogeneous group and that material review and large-concept discussion are most appropriately addressed in a homogeneous grouping.[16] This could naturally describe the difference between the private lesson and the group or studio class.

WRITING EXERCISE: Reflect in writing on how you would sensitively create homogeneous groups in a piano studio. What characteristics would you look for in students? What activities would you assign to these homogenous groups?

STRATEGIES FOR WORKING WITH GIFTED STUDENTS

In their review of research concerning teaching gifted students in a detracked classroom, Johnsen and Ryser[17] describe five areas for differentiating instruction, as follows:

1. Modifying content
2. Allowing for student preferences in instructional areas
3. Altering the pace of instructional delivery
4. Creating a flexible classroom environment
5. Using specific instructional strategies

Furthermore, these researchers provide the following suggestions for instructional strategies for gifted students:

1. Posing open-ended questions that require higher-level thinking
2. Modeling thinking strategies, including decision making and evaluation
3. Accepting ideas and suggestions from students and expanding upon them
4. Making original and independent problems and solutions possible
5. Helping students identify rules, principles, and relationships
6. Taking time to explain the nature of specific errors

Having students analyze their repertoire pieces from a harmonic perspective is an excellent way to engage their higher-level thinking. Having them make guesses about what comes next in a piece by Mozart based on the previous pieces by Mozart that they have learned would be an effective way to model thinking strategies and evaluation. Having a student provide a theme for a "theme and variations" composition project collaboratively written with the teacher would be an outstanding use of the concept of original and independent problems. As you can see, the enrichment activities available to a piano teacher based on differentiated instruction are many and varied.

WRITING EXERCISE: Write an enrichment activity for a group of gifted piano students in your studio based on Johnson and Ryser's five areas for differentiating instruction.

Westberg et al. completed a case study of teachers in elementary schools that were well known for meeting the needs of gifted students.[18] In their case study, the researchers noted that the following were the most frequently used strategies:

- The early establishment of high standards
- Making modifications to the curriculum
- Finding mentors for students
- Encouraging independent investigations and projects
- Creating flexible instructional groups

These best practices have important implications for piano teachers. An environment of support coupled with high standards from the very beginning of a child's musical training can help set the tone for a discipline of practice and commitment when the plasticity of a child's brain is the greatest.

ESTABLISHING AN EFFECTIVE LEARNING ENVIRONMENT FOR GIFTED STUDENTS

Effective instructional differentiation is most successfully obtained in a physical classroom and learning climate that are both flexible and supportive. An effective teacher of all students, but in particular gifted students, attempts to maintain a relaxed and still challenging environment in which responsibility and autonomy are encouraged, different students' needs are met, and students' strengths are celebrated.

The teacher in a differentiated learning environment understands the importance of creating a hybrid educational setting that builds on the strengths of classroom-wide activities as well as individual ones. The private piano studio is a natural fit for such a blend of educational opportunities. Research recommends what are known as *anchor activities*, tasks that students can work on with little to no supervision.[19] In the piano studio, these tasks may include working on an iPad application for music theory while waiting for a lesson to begin, listening assignments completed at home with associated journal responses, and composition, improvisation, or other creative assignments to be completed outside the piano lesson. Because these anchor activities will naturally be completed almost entirely independently, it is important that students are given a clear opportunity to get help when they need it. The advent of such social media formats as Facebook and Twitter gives students the ability to communicate with their teacher should they need help.

CREATING AN EFFECTIVE EMOTIONAL ENVIRONMENT FOR GIFTED STUDENTS

A comfortable, nonthreatening learning environment is important for all students, including gifted learners. High-ability students are frequently perfectionists, which, in the context of the learning of an instrument, may mean that they place particular significance on perfect performances in recitals, competitions, and even lessons and studio classes. Gifted learners may occasionally find themselves to be social outcasts because of their unusual abilities. Some may be used to having a higher status than others in a piano studio. The foundation of an effective learning environment is a feeling of safety and acceptance by peers and teachers. A piano teacher can help create this atmosphere by modeling respect and care for all members of his or her studio, as well as for the students of other studios in a given geographic location. Every piano student needs to recognize and value his or her abilities and those of peers. Gifted students may sometimes feel insecure when they are presented with open-ended problem-solving activities. For example, a piano teacher may feel that a gifted student is more likely to be able to learn a repertoire assignment independently, without the detailed instruction that another student may require. Some gifted students may insist that they need instructions and procedures specifically laid out so that they can follow directions exactly and "perform it perfectly every time." A teacher of gifted students should remind pupils that mistakes are perhaps the most important part of the learning process and should realize that because mistakes may be few and far between for the gifted student they may be particularly painful. Gifted students may also resist showing their work, or, in the case of learning an instrument, resist the step-by-step process that is required of nearly everyone. For example, they may not see the utility in a discipline of working on Hanon exercises or on scales and arpeggios when they are able to easily execute passages like these in the pieces they are learning. Explaining the value of rudiments to gifted students by using something like a scoring guide or specific rubric in a student's homework notebook can help a teacher communicate the importance of activities that a student may feel are boring.

SUPPORTING GIFTED FEMALES

Gifted female students face challenges that their male counterparts do not, and these can undermine their abilities and potential. Research shows that gifted girls do not achieve at expected levels in middle school and high school and that they often do not pursue careers that are considered typically prestigious by society.[20] A number of reasons have been identified for female students' underachievement, including societal gender stereotypes, a lack of role models, declining confidence in their exceptional abilities, conflicting expectations from teachers and parents, and pressure from peers to hide their abilities and intelligence.[21] Research has also shown that teachers often have less tolerance for girls who call out answers in class out of turn, ask numerous questions, and are confident in their opinions and willing to argue. These behaviors are more likely to be accepted as evidence of giftedness in boys.[22] Because of these numerous forces, girls occasionally tend to downplay their intelligence in order to conform to what they may perceive as society's accepted stereotype of femininity.[23] To battle the issues that work against the achievement level of gifted girls, it is critical that teachers and students become aware of their biases about gender. Some helpful tactics for teachers working with gifted girls include the following:

- Pointing out specific examples of their excellent work, while correcting them when they attribute their accomplishments exclusively to luck or to hard work. In the case of a gifted female pianist, a teacher should be sure to attribute her successes to both practice discipline and native musical talent.
- Providing opportunities for gifted girls to use their leadership abilities. Actively recruiting a deserving gifted girl to the top leadership post in your local music club could pay big dividends in terms of helping her break down society's idea that such a leadership position is best filled by a male.
- Exposing a gifted piano student to female mentors in powerful positions. Seek out the female dean of your nearest college or conservatory to see if she will serve as a mentor for your gifted female student.
- Discussing gender stereotypes with your female students, as well as the mixed messages that society transmits about femininity, intelligence, and achievement.
- Encouraging all of your students to research and report on women's contributions to music in the roles of composer, performer, conductor, and leader.

The opportunity to work with gifted students is both a blessing and a challenge that requires a piano teacher to actively pursue types of instruction that support and stir such students. Knowledge of these tactics, as well as knowledge of the specific emotional needs of gifted students and the traps that they face, can help a teacher be as supportive as possible when working in this capacity.

NOTES

1. Robert J. Sternberg, "What Should Intelligence Tests Test? Implications of a Triarchic Theory of Intelligence for Intelligence Testing," *Educational Researcher* 13, no. 1 (1984): 5–15.
2. Howard Gardner, *Multiple Intelligences: New Horizons*, rev. ed. (New York: Basic Books, 2006).
3. David Perkins, *Outsmarting IQ: The Emerging Science of Learnable Intelligence* (New York: Simon and Schuster, 1995).
4. Joseph S. Renzulli, "The Three Ring Conception of Giftedness: A Developmental Model for Creative Productivity." *Gifted Child Quarterly* 20 (1984): 303–305.
5. Donna Y. Ford, "The Underrepresentation of Minority Students in Gifted Education: Problems and Promises in Recruitment and Retention," *Journal of Special Education* 32, no. 1 (1998): 4–14.
6. Renate Nummela Caine and Geoffrey Caine, *Making Connections: Teaching and the Human Brain* (Alexandria, VA: Association for Supervision and Curriculum Development, 1991).
7. Wolfram Schultz, Peter Dayan, and P. Read Montague, "A Neural Substrate of Prediction and Reward," *Science* 275, no. 5306 (1997): 1593–1599.
8. Sally M. Reis and Jeanne H. Purcell, "An Analysis of Content Elimination and Strategies Used by Elementary Classroom Teachers in the Curriculum Compacting Process," *Journal for the Education of the Gifted* 16, no. 2 (1993): 147–170.
9. Edwin E. Gordon, "All about Audiation and Music Aptitudes: Edwin E. Gordon Discusses Using Audiation and Music Aptitudes as Teaching Tools to Allow Students to Reach Their Full Music Potential," *Music Educators Journal* 86, no. 2 (1999): 41–44.
10. Edwin E. Gordon, "A Factor Analysis of the Musical Aptitude Profile, the Primary Measures of Music Audiation, and the Intermediate Measures of Music Audiation," *Bulletin of the Council for Research in Music Education* (1986): 17–25.

11. Edwin E. Gordon, *Iowa Tests of Music Literacy: Manual* (Chicago: GIA Publications, 2001).
12. Cindy Dooley, "The Challenge: Meeting the Needs of Gifted Readers," *Reading Teacher* 46, no. 7 (1993): 546–551.
13. Karen B. Rogers, "Grouping the Gifted and Talented: Questions and Answers," *Roeper Review* 16, no. 1 (1993): 8–12.
14. Karen B. Rogers, "Using Current Research to Make "Good" Decisions about Grouping," *NASSP Bulletin* 82, no. 595 (1998): 38–46.
15. Adam Gamoran and Matthew Weinstein, "Differentiation and Opportunity in Restructured Schools," *American Journal of Education* 106, no. 3 (1998): 385–415.
16. Adams-Byers, Jan, Sara Squiller Whitsell, and Sidney M. Moon. "Gifted Students' Perceptions of the Academic and Social/Emotional Effects of Homogeneous and Heterogeneous Grouping." *Gifted Child Quarterly* 48, no. 1 (2004): 53.
17. Susan K. Johnsen "Johnson." and Gail R. Ryser, "An Overview of Effective Practices with Gifted Students in General-Education Settings," *Journal for the Education of the Gifted* 19, no. 4 (1996): 379–404.
18. Karen L. Westberg, Francis X. Archambault, Sally M. Dobyns, and Thomas J. Salvin, "An Observational Study of Instructional and Curricular Practices Used with Gifted and Talented Students." In *Regular Classrooms*. Research Monograph 93104. (Storrs: University of Connecticut, National Research Center on the Gifted and Talented, 1993): 41–44.
19. Tonya R. Moon, Carolyn M. Callahan, and Carol A. Tomlinson, "The Effects of Mentoring Relationships on Preservice Teachers' Attitudes Toward Academically Diverse Students," *Gifted Child Quarterly* 43, no. 2 (1999): 56–62.
20. Leigh A. Badolato, "Recognizing and Meeting the Special Needs of Gifted Females," *Gifted Child Today* 21, no. 6 (1998): 32.
21. Joan Franklin Smutny and Rita Haynes Blocksom, *Education of the Gifted: Programs and Perspectives* (Bloomington: Phi Delta Kappa Educational Foundation, 1990). http://www.worldcat.org/search?qt=worldcat_org_all&q=Education+of+the+Gifted%3A+Programs+and+Perspectives.
22. Marie F. Shoffner and Deborah W. Newsome, "Identity Development of Gifted Female Adolescents: The Influence of Career Development, Age, and Life-Role Salience," *Journal of Secondary Gifted Education* 12, no. 4 (2001): 201–211.
23. Julianne Jacob Ryan, "Exploring the Need for Specialized Counseling for Gifted Females," *Gifted Child Today* 22, no. 5 (1999): 14–17.

Chapter 3

Teaching Adult Pianists

In the field of education, adult students, sometimes called adult learners or mature learners, are typically defined as individuals who are twenty-five years of age and older.[1] In the United States, adult students are categorized as nontraditional students who must meet at least one of the following six criteria according to the National Center for Education Statistics. Such a student

1. delays enrollment (does not enter post-secondary education in the same calendar year in which he or she finished high school)
2. attends part-time for at least part of the academic year
3. works full-time (thirty-five hours or more per week) while enrolled
4. is considered financially independent for the purposes of determining eligibility for financial aid
5. has dependents other than a spouse (usually children, but sometimes other dependents)
6. does not have a high school diploma (completed high school with a GED or other high school completion certificate or did not finish high school)[2]

These criteria do not necessarily apply to adult piano students, but they certainly create a potential profile of such pupils. Adult students, particularly those who are coming to the study of the instrument as beginners or amateurs, have a specific set of needs that teachers should do their best to address. This chapter aims to illustrate the concerns of adult beginner-to-intermediate piano students, as well as give tactics for providing instruction for them that will be effective, exciting, and challenging for both student and teacher.

Adult students of beginning piano are frequently encountered in higher education. Community colleges, schools and colleges of music, and music conservatories may offer group and individual instruction for the adult beginner taught by members of the faculty or graduate assistants. The Michigan State University College of Music, for example, offers a class titled MUS 147, a group course for beginning piano students from across the campus taught by the author as a demonstration and laboratory experience for students in the master of music program in piano pedagogy. This course is always at capacity and usually runs with a wait list of between five and ten students. I believe that the demand for this course is indicative of the demand for such courses in the academy. In my experience, students are eager for these types of courses, not as "easy A's" but, rather, as a significant academic challenge or artistic outlet. I have consistently found this population of students to be among the most eager and appreciative of the various populations of undergraduate and graduate students I have worked with.

The number of adult learners, based on the definitions established above, is overtaking the number of traditional college students between the ages of eighteen and twenty-two in higher education settings. In a 2002 paper the National Center for Education Statistics noted that nearly three-quarters of American undergraduates met one of the criteria listed above for classification as nontraditional students. Of those, 46 percent were defined as such because of delayed enrollment.[3] While this more classical definition of the adult learner certainly differs from that of the college-aged non-music-major beginner, similarities exist, especially when one compares the delay of music study in these students to the delay in general post-secondary adult learners. Teachers of college-aged students not majoring in music can glean much from the body of research that exists about adult learners in general.

Because adult learners have lived and learned for much longer periods of time than have children or adolescents, the variety of learning experiences among adult learners is much greater than among younger populations. Consider the diversity amongst adults within your social circle: Some work, some are retired. Some have significant academic training, some have very little. Some adults have family and dependent obligations, some do not. Some are married, and some are single. Their vocations vary widely as well.

MOTIVATION IN ADULT PIANISTS

Adult learners tend to have different levels of motivation than do younger learners, and especially more varied sources of motivation. Adults may be motivated to play the piano because of childhood artistic goals not met or regrets about quitting the piano at a young age. They may wish to study the instrument for opportunities to perform in a church or with friends, or for opportunities to connect with a child of theirs who has taken up the piano. Other reasons include stress relief and artistic pursuit. While all of these (and many more) are worthy in their own way, they all represent external motivations. Unlike those of young children, which may revolve around the attainment of prizes or participation in recitals and competitions, the external motivations of adults may more typically be based on opportunities and personal goal setting. Usually, the motivational construct of piano teaching concerns shifting from the realm of external motivations to that of internal motivations; this may be less necessary in the teaching of adults, whose external motivations are based on a longer, richer, and more complex life experience. This is not to say that internal motivation and a love of the instrument are not worthy in themselves, but in adults, motivation to learn may be more mature and well thought-out, as well as self-initiated. Furthermore, adult students are likely financing their study themselves. However cynical this viewpoint may be, financial investment in any kind of pursuit can be a powerful factor in encouraging hard work.

CHALLENGES FACED BY ADULT LEARNERS

The physiological aspects of aging can affect the success of an adult learner because of the typical deterioration in physical status including overall health, energy, vision, and hearing. Although a college-aged beginning student may not necessarily be faced with deteriorating health and physical skills, the sophisticated physical challenges and fine motor skills and control required for piano study may be difficult to attain for an adult student, especially when cognitive ability may far outweigh ability to learn new physical movements. Perhaps the overarching challenge of teaching adult beginning students lies directly in this dichotomy between diminished physical ease and the advanced cognitive state of the adult brain. One of the most powerful and important parts of teaching young children the piano is the matching of the learning of advanced physical skills in large and small muscle groups and the rapid cognitive growth on a biological level in the young person's brain. The absence of this pairing in the adult learner can lead to frustration. Adults may be able to understand the concept of the fingering pattern for the D-flat major scale, but be less easily able to execute such a pattern at a quick tempo. Teachers should have tools at their disposal for dealing with such frustrations and should be understanding when they occur, knowing that much of this difficulty is based on the biological realities of the adult brain and the physiological realities of the adult body.

An adult may bring many more psychosocial pressures to the learning environment than a child would. Although it would be naïve to say that a child enters the learning environment as a blank slate, free of the pressures of the social environment, these sorts of pressures may be heightened in the adult learner. Cognitive differences between adult learners may be much more stark than in children and adolescents. With a lifetime of learning (or a lifetime of a lack of learning), the adult student population most likely will exhibit a greater variability in cognitive and educational abilities. Furthermore, personality in adults is typically fully formed and seasoned, whereas personality is still forming in children and adolescents. In addition to the great amount of variability in the personalities of adults, the impact that personality traits may have on the success or failure of piano study may be more powerful than it would be for children. Adults who are naturally introspective and reticent about performing in public may have a harder time breaking out of such a mold through the experiential learning that is gained by performance opportunities. For the adult who is shy, the offer of a public performance may simply be a nonstarter, whereas a shy child might be convinced to give it a try. Socioeconomic factors may also have a strong impact on the educational success of the adult student. Such factors do have an impact on children, but children have an incredible way of ignoring or not seeing such factors in their lives, while *just being children*. The adult, on the other hand, is faced with the pressures of his or her socioeconomic level, whether it is the college student who must work outside jobs to pay the rent while other students are practicing or the adult who is living paycheck to paycheck and struggling to justify the seeming luxury of private piano instruction. Such factors are typically at the forefront of the adult's mind, and the positive or negative impact of these stressors can have a tremendous effect on an adult student's ability to succeed.

Although there are many challenges in teaching adult learners, one of the great advantages is the fact that they, with more life experience and cognitive development and skills than children and adolescents, are able to infer deeper meanings from those experiences. The ability and willingness of adults to apply even abstract concepts gained in their piano study to larger experiences in their lives make the teaching of adult learners very satisfying.

STRATEGIES FOR TEACHING ADULT PIANISTS

Teaching adult pianists can be a very natural exercise when one considers that communication between adults is much freer and more natural than that between an adult and a child. Children communicate on a wholly different level than do adults. Children typically are not constrained by traditionally established social norms of engagement, the boundary between fantasy and reality is much thinner for them, and their willingness to tell stories and exhibit verbal creativity can be quite remarkable. For the teacher, adopting and adapting to the language and communication characteristics of a child can be a pursuit unto itself. When an adult teaches an adult, an inherent naturalness in the dialogue ensues in the course of a lesson. When peers speak to one another, conversation takes place, rather than lecture-style instruction or adoption of a more childlike mode of speech. It might even be said that an aura of friendship may be a desirable outcome of a piano lesson with an adult learner. Conversing naturally with an adult student may create at atmosphere of mutual respect, trust, and comfort that will help learning unfold with ease. That being said, the peer relationship that an adult teacher may have with an adult student may create some dangers that teachers of adult students need to consider. In the course of a lesson, for example, the conversation may easily veer into personal matters. There is no formula here. The effective teacher should take the lead from the student regarding how much personal information and narrative is comfortable and appropriate. The adult student may find great value in having a confidant in a piano teacher. Pairing these sorts of services with learning that is driven by the needs of the student can be a tremendously powerful paradigm of instruction.

The piano teacher will benefit from quickly learning the specific personalities of adult students. Some will be particularly inquisitive and may wish to gain knowledge by expressing curiosity and having dialogue. Others may prefer to know how to complete an assignment on a much more concrete and specific level. Other students may simply wish to study the piano for their own pleasure and personal well-being. All of these types should be understood and respected. Furthermore, effective teachers should seek to identify students' personalities quickly and accurately.

While enjoyment in music making should be a goal for all piano teaching, perhaps this goal should be at the forefront of curricular design for adult students. In interviews, amateur adult musicians and non-music-major college-aged students mentioned such concepts as enjoyment, pleasure, and relaxation as motivations to study piano. Driver and Bruns examined the field of leisure-benefit research in adults and made useful discoveries that should be noted and possibly implemented in the practice of teaching adult piano students. These researchers cited the categories of personal benefits, social and cultural benefits, economic benefits, and environmental benefits as driving factors in the selection of leisure and hobby activities by adults.[4] When a teacher of adult students considers the many benefits of the study of piano, the following may have particular importance for their resonance with the categories listed above.

Fun, enjoyment, and pleasure. Perhaps at a basic level, we as humans seek out activities in every aspect of our lives that might fit these particular categories. Whether in the choice of our hobbies, our food, our friends, the use of our vacation time, or, if we are fortunate, our vocation, we attempt to participate in activities that bring a smile to our faces. The lives of adults often are filled with activities that do not satisfy these wishes. Because of stresses from a job, a romantic relationship, caring for aging parents, or financial difficulties and anxiety, adulthood is often challenging and taxing. Providing a means of fun, enjoyment, and pleasure to an adult student can keep him or her coming back week after week.

Self-esteem. Although adults are often past the stage of identity formation that takes place during adolescence, the development and nurturing of self-esteem can still play a significant role in motivating the adult piano student. To put it bluntly, adulthood can be a humiliating experience. As my child's brilliant first-grade teacher once said to me at the end of a particularly trying day with some of the students in her class, "Don't you just love constantly being told that you are doing something wrong?" Adults who have children, and those who work with children, have a tremendous responsibility for the well-being of these young people as it relates to their safety, their health and well-being, their training, or their emotional learning.

Leading this noble kind of life requires a great amount of selflessness and generosity that almost never ceases. Providing a challenging outlet for an adult amateur student or college-aged non-major can create the conditions for goal achievement, and such a direct reflection of the student's hard work and dedication can lead to great gains in self-esteem.

Relaxation. There is something to be said for sitting down at the instrument with a glass of wine after a long and stressful day at work. As professional musicians who are typically spending long hours at the piano to prepare music that is required by some sort of deadline, this feeling may be something that we have lost touch with. Never underestimate the power of a student studying the piano for pleasure, and for pleasure only. When working with a student for whom this motivation ranks high, the selection of repertoire is of primary importance. Although with most students we may seek to advance skill by offering challenges that are always one step ahead of their current ability level, allowing adult students who value the sheer pleasure of music making to stay firmly and comfortably within a specific difficulty level may pay dividends in terms of their enjoyment, their motivation, and their love of the study of their instrument.

Self-expression. Music is a uniquely expressive pursuit. In many ways, we all have the ability to enjoy the sounds of most kinds of classical music, and we all have the ability to understand much of music's inner workings when they are explained and demonstrated in an accessible way. I suppose the same could be said of the visual arts, but there seems to be something more basically human about music in terms of its connection to all people. We don't typically interact with great visual art daily, yet almost all of us interact with great musical art daily. Because of this commonality, music can serve as a very easy way into self-expression for an adult student who may not have the opportunity to express himself or herself in the daily grind. Understanding the importance of self-expression as a potential motivating factor for the adult student might help the teacher design activities that tap into the concept of creativity, in particular. Teachers should strive to utilize the areas of composition and improvisation for adult students of varying levels in order to "scratch the itch" of self-expression that is in all of us, especially adult amateur students.

In my experience, adults also frequently cite the concepts of accomplishment, personal satisfaction, and the attainment of skills applicable to a performance setting (in a place of worship, for example).

WRITING EXERCISE: Develop a motivation survey for your adult students. Include at least ten possible motivating factors for them to choose from. Write about the curricular implications that various answers to these questions might have. In particular, consider the types of repertoire you might choose for adult students based on their answers.

THE BENEFITS OF PIANO STUDY FOR ADULTS

In addition to motivation, it is important to consider the benefits of piano study in order to more fully understand the reasons why adults might undertake it. Peter Jutras, professor of piano and piano pedagogy at the University of Georgia, undertook significant scientific research on this topic in his article "The Benefits of Adult Piano Study as Self-Reported by Selected Adult Piano Students."[5] In Jutras's study, adult piano students from all geographic regions of the United States completed a questionnaire listing thirty-one individual benefits. They were organized into three categories: "Personal

Benefits," "Skill Benefits," and "Social/Cultural Benefits." Students indicated whether each benefit related to them and rated the importance of each on a scale of 1 to 10. Results of this questionnaire showed that the category "Skill Benefits" was the most often agreed-on and highest rated in the study, with more than 90 percent of respondents marking yes for each of the seven skill benefits. The category "Personal Benefits" was also quite highly rated, in particular, benefits related to self-actualization and fun. Personal benefits related to the self received moderate ratings. Personal benefits that might be described as tied to introversion, including Imagination/Creativity, Spirituality, and Aesthetic Appreciation, were lower-rated benefits. As a category the social/cultural benefits were the lowest-rated benefits and thus considered the least important in the study. Of all benefits listed, the most often marked yes were Skill Improvement, Musical Knowledge, Musicianship, Accomplishment, Skill Refinement, Technique, Play/Fun, Escape from Routine, and Music Listening. The highest-rated benefits in terms of importance were Dream Fulfilled, Technique, Accomplishment, Escape from Routine, Skill Improvement, Musicianship, Musical Knowledge, Play/Fun, Skill Refinement, and Personal Growth.

When one surveys the list of highly rated and frequently occurring benefits from the Jutras study, it is clear that certain categories of benefits come from similar groups of motivations. Adult piano students do not have a homogenous view of the benefits of piano study. In other words, they are not all simply looking to have fun or to find an outlet or relief from stresses in other parts of their lives. The benefits Dream Fulfilled and Accomplishment seem to speak to the fact that many adult pianists are looking to achieve significant, often long-held goals at the instrument. These students may be very serious about their study, working diligently and without respite between lessons. These may also be the students who wish to be particularly challenged in terms of repertoire and may even have a list of pieces that they have always wanted to play. The wishes of such students should be honored and respected, but a teacher should also be cautious about being an arbiter for what a given student is truly able to succeed at and what might be a futile pursuit or a frustrating exercise. An adult student who has always wanted to perform the third concerto of Rachmaninoff but has not formally studied piano for twenty years might be on the right track when it comes to knowing the type of music that speaks to him or her and makes him or her want to come to the piano day after day. Yet the technical, physical, and musical demands of such a piece would be inappropriate for nearly every adult student who might fit this profile. Harnessing the student's excitement for this work might result in a teacher's suggesting a series of Rachmaninoff preludes that would satisfy the cravings that the student might have for lush harmony, long, penetrating melodies filled with melancholy, and dense pianistic textures that place significant demands on the performer while requiring the performer to invest tremendous time and effort at the keyboard. The appropriateness of this music is seen in its shorter format, its more manageable text, and its musically more straightforward form.

The positive response to the benefits Skill Improvement, Musical Knowledge, Skill Refinement, and Technique may speak to the fact that many adult students find that practical and tangible benefits brought about by high-level piano instruction and study are critical and worth seeking out. These are the students who might be part-time pianists or organists at their church, who might use the piano or keyboard in their place of work (as an employee of a retirement home or as a school teacher), or who might be seeking specific functional skills when it comes to utilizing the piano more effectively in their own home as their family gathers around the instrument to sing Christmas carols. Students who identify these benefits as important dividends of their musical study may find particular value in arranging skills, tactics for harmonizing melodies in interesting and new ways, and improved sight-reading capability.

Finally, the benefits Play/Fun and Escape from Routine speak to what I described above as particular motivators for adult students. When viewed as a benefit, the concept of providing adult students with an enjoyable outlet from the pressures of life is justified. These are the students who may love playing the piano but who may play more often when their day has been particularly challenging. They value the ability to continually review repertoire that is comfortable and has been worked on for a long time. These students might not be eager to move forward with their pianistic skill set but may be content with and even excited about the prospect of having a large repertoire of manageable and tuneful pieces to play. Furthermore, these are the students who may value the role of listener that a teacher often plays, for they consider the opportunity to converse with a peer during their lessons as important as or more valuable than piano study itself. Teachers should respect and hone this role, although it is somewhat nontraditional.

Adult learners and college-aged non-major students have diverse motivations and perceptions of the benefits of piano study. This diversity is a strength and an exciting aspect of the profiles of these types of students, but at the same time, research has shown patterns in what adult students value in piano instruction. The savvy piano teacher will become aware of the various impacts of adult piano study. Doing so will not only assist the teacher in better serving current piano students but will benefit the teacher in terms of the entrepreneurial possibilities of teaching adult students. Word of mouth among adult friends spreads fast in terms of pursuits and hobbies that people are enjoying. Being the beneficiary of such good buzz can prove to be quite lucrative for the curious piano teacher.

CONSIDERING ADULT LEARNERS BY AGE GROUP

Adulthood is typically marked by significant differences in priorities through the decades. For example, many individuals in their twenties may still belong to the world of "emerging adulthood," that is, a sort of extended adolescence, while some individuals in their forties may be young grandparents. Michelle Conda, an expert in the field of piano andragogy, outlines some of these differences in her excellent article "The Joys of Teaching Music: What I Have Learned from My Adult Students," which appeared in *American Music Teacher*.[6] Conda uses her experiences as a teacher of adults to describe some of these challenges according to age group. Some characteristics and strategies are highlighted below.

The twenties. Conda describes these millennial students as having much of their adult life ahead of them. Typically, marriage and children are still in their future. These students may be new to the workforce and may have more disposable income to use on activities like music that give them an emotional outlet.

The thirties. According to Conda, these students are very busy working to find their mission in life. Many adult students in their thirties are starting families and attempting to become leaders in their communities. Conda describes the difficulties in getting this group of students committed to regular piano study when they are often torn between that and many other commitments in their lives.

The forties. Many students in their forties may be more established in their careers than students in their thirties. Students in their forties have learned to express themselves effectively. Conda describes them as having the ability to use music to express emotions and fulfill emotional needs. This group of students may find the multiple affections of music (sad, angry, happy) satisfying. Moreover, students in their forties are typically in a period of transitions such as their children leaving home and their parents passing away.

The fifties. Conda describes typical students in their fifties as "self-assured and not afraid." She also notes the importance of specific goal-setting during this decade, as this type of careful planning can help keep students on task when they are often eager to dive into an artistic pursuit that may be new to them. In addition, physical changes that may result in difficulties at the instrument may creep in during this decade, including arthritis and hearing loss.

These characteristics may not pertain to every student in these age groups, but they give a glimpse into the diversity of experiences that learners in multiple age groups bring to the piano. Considering these differences can assist the teacher greatly in developing effective curricula for students of various ages.

NOTES

1. Southern Regional Education Board. "Who Is the Adult Learner?" Accessed March 3, 2018. https://www.sreb.org/general-information/who-adult-learner.
2. National Center for Education Statistics, "Nontraditional Undergraduates: Definitions and Data." Accessed April 18, 2017. https://nces.ed.gov/pubs/web/97578e.asp.
3. Susan Choy, "Nontraditional Undergraduates (NCES 2002–012)" (Washington, DC: U.S. Department of Education, 2002).
4. Beverley L. Driver and Donald H. Bruns, "Concepts and Uses of the Benefits Approach to Leisure," *Leisure Studies* (1999): 349–369.
5. Peter J. Jutras, "The Benefits of Adult Piano Study as Self-Reported by Selected Adult Piano Students," *Journal of Research in Music Education* 54, no. 2 (2006): 97–110.
6. Michelle Conda, "The Joys of Teaching Music: What I Have Learned from My Adult Students," *American Music Teacher* 59, no. 2 (2009): 30–32.

Chapter 4

Meeting the Needs of the Recreational Student

Music study has value for everyone. The music teacher has a critical role in society that goes well beyond preparing, or hoping to prepare, musicians of artist caliber. Music study has impacts that extend past easily demonstrated improvement and knowledge of artistic goals to touch on skills related to focus, problem solving, time management, teamwork, empathy, cultural awareness, confidence building, the development of style, refinement of motor skills, stress relief, and myriad other benefits. To restrict these benefits to students who wish to become professionals would border on selfishness. Music teachers have a responsibility to make their expertise known to a greater proportion of society and to place their skills squarely in the center of a community's arena of consciousness, making themselves available to anyone wishing to benefit from music's deep well of advantages. Access to music performances, recordings, and creation is more widely available today than at any time in history. People have the opportunity to compose, perform, and record music instantly in their homes with the advent of relatively inexpensive and easy-to-use technology. Traditional forms of musical access remain including family music making, individual music classes and lessons, community and church ensembles, terrestrial and satellite radio, television broadcasts, and commercial recordings, now easily available by streaming over the Internet, sometimes at no charge to the listener. These more traditional avenues of access are now expanding to include music-based gaming and real-time interactive music instruction via digital communication using digital musical instruments. With such unprecedented access to music, and with the universally accepted human love of and admiration for music, why is it that so much of society holds such a low view of the social and political importance of music and music study? This is a far larger question than this book can possibly address, but perhaps the answer lies somewhere in the world of recreational music making (RMM), considering the significant and easily recognized societal impacts that this type of teaching could have. In this chapter, I outline the different categories of RMM, as well as approaches to teaching students who might self-identify as recreational. I also highlight research, mostly from the medical and eldercare fields, to create a body of justification for the importance of including RMM in your teaching studio.

A HISTORY OF RECREATIONAL MUSIC MAKING

Karl T. Bruhn is widely recognized as the father of the music making and wellness movement, which later came to me known as RMM. As a former senior vice president of marketing at Yamaha Corporation of America, Bruhn visualized a system of music making for all people. Before 2006, RMM was not much more than a loose idea discussed briefly at state and national piano teaching conferences. Now it is one of the main topics for presentations and discussions at many of the top conferences for piano teaching internationally. The National Association of Music Merchants (NAMM) has emerged as a champion of the movement and distributes grants to RMM programs annually. Bruhn defined RMM as follows:

> RMM encompasses enjoyable, accessible and fulfilling group music-based activities that unite people of all ages regardless of their challenges, backgrounds, ethnicity, ability, or prior experience. From exercise, nurturing, social support, bonding and spirituality, to intellectual stimulation, heightened understanding and enhanced capacity to cope with life challenges, the benefits of RMM extend far beyond music. RMM ultimately affords unparalleled creative expression that unites our bodies, minds and spirits.[1]

Brenda Dillon defines RMM at the piano as "music making for the joy of it in non-stressful environments."[2] Dillon and Brian Chung state that "Recreational Music Making was founded upon the following principles: All people should experience the joy and benefits of music making; music making can be enjoyed without stress and performance requirements; music making can nurture the whole person and improve quality of life; and music making is beneficial to the health of the participant."[3] Dillon has also discussed how "the requirements of traditional teaching" can bring about "pressure and frustration" because of busy lifestyles. According to Dillon, "In traditional piano teaching, primary emphasis is placed on achieving a high level of performance. A structured curriculum is employed. Teaching occurs primarily through private/individual lessons. The teacher prescribes the direction and style of the lesson. The teacher appraises the student's level of success."

Dillon argues that implementing some of the attributes of the RMM style of teaching may "not only transform the music teaching profession, but also elevate the importance and impact of music making in our culture." Dillon and Chung describe the characteristics of RMM as follows: "Performance is not emphasized or required. The curriculum can bend and adapt at any time. Teaching occurs primarily in *group* lessons. The student and teacher participate *together* in prescribing the direction/style of lessons. Students learn from the teacher *and* other class members. The *student* appraises the level of success."[4]

Perhaps the most important aspect of RMM is the accessibility of music study to any beginning piano student, regardless of age or musical aptitude. An adult beginner may feel that he or she is a success from the first lesson simply by having an encouraging and positive facilitator with a sense of humor. Karl T. Bruhn draws an important distinction between a teacher and a facilitator, "Teachers," he writes, "often lead students to the teacher's goals, while facilitators walk beside the student and guide the way to the student's goals. The objective is to have students realize a great deal of success from the very beginning."[5] Aspects of being a facilitator, as identified by Bruhn, would be important characteristics for any teacher to possess, whether teaching in a recreational music setting or in what might be thought of as a more traditional setting. Brenda Dillon indicates that an instructor may reduce the stress of classes by encouraging students to let go of typical expectations of progress, writing, "I know that human beings have an affinity for learning certain skills, but I think you can learn to do almost anything if you are willing to devote the time and attention to it. With every new class, I urge them to remove the word talent from their vocabulary. I tell them the formula for learning to play the piano is simply: Desire + Slow Repetition = Success."[6]

Performance can be a stress-inducing activity for a student of any level. Typically, performance is not required in the study of RMM. Informality during performance opportunities for students of RMM is a tactic worth trying in order to draw students who might be reluctant in stressful situations into the world of performance.

In addition to strategies for normalizing and reducing the stress of performance, choosing repertoire in specific and wise ways is also critical to the successful teaching of RMM. Dillon states the following in regard to choosing repertoire for recreational music students: "When it comes to learning to read music, I find that adults are primarily interested in learning to play pieces they have always yearned to play. That goes hand-in-hand with my belief that mastering music fundamentals will lead adults to that promised land of fulfilling their dreams."

Teaching RMM in groups or classes, either on two pianos or in a piano lab with multiple electronic keyboards, can be advantageous for this sort of teaching endeavor. The social aspect of such an instructional setting may improve the learning atmosphere and give students an opportunity to hear other students perform and be taught. Developing a relationship with a piano retailer may be mutually advantageous: Teachers may gain a setting in which to teach, and piano retailers may develop relationships with potential clients in the students of a recreational music class who may be at a point in their lives when their expendable income may more easily be used on a piano.

Many experts in the field of RMM emphasize the need for the teacher to facilitate learning and to pace and adjust the progress of a class according to student feedback. Such tactics, while useful in all teaching, are a driving force behind effective curriculum organization in RMM.

RESEARCH INTO RECREATIONAL MUSIC MAKING

In their article "Recreational Music-Making: An Integrative Group Intervention for Reducing Burnout and Improving Mood State in First-Year Associate Degree Nursing Students; Insights and Economic Impact," Barry Bittman, Karl T. Bruhn, and colleagues describe a study in which they measured the impact of a six-session RMM protocol on burnout and mood dimensions as well as total mood disturbance on nursing students.[7] The authors note that burnout and negative mood states are particular problems in the world of undergraduate nursing education. The authors state that these particular issues lead to alarming rates of academic and career attrition. According to the literature, attrition not only reduces the number of employable nurses but also has other serious consequences, including feelings of failure among those who leave nursing school, the burden of a substantial loan debt, and "burnout," that is, emotional and physical depletion or deterioration in response to excessive work demands. When this paper was published, 7.5 percent of male nurses and 4.1 percent of female nurses in the United States were leaving the profession within four years of graduation, compared to only 2 percent of men and 2.7 percent of women ten years earlier. In addition, 40 percent of hospital nurses had burnout levels that exceeded the norms for healthcare workers, while job dissatisfaction was four times greater than the average for all U.S. workers.

Motivated by these statistics, the researchers set out to measure the impact of RMM on beginning nursing students. Specifically, a six-session, cost-effective group-based RMM protocol was provided to nursing students at the start of their clinical education with the hope that it would result in diminished burnout and total mood disturbance. The authors point out that "burnout" is a syndrome comprised of three well-documented variables—emotional exhaustion, depersonalization, and reduced personal accomplishment—that occurs among individuals who work with people in some capacity. In this study, Group Empowerment Drumming, a comprehensive, well-established RMM protocol, was utilized. Nursing students used hand drums and a variety of auxiliary percussion instruments including bells and maracas. Groups of nursing students met with a trained facilitator at a designated time for a total of six one-hour weekly sessions. Each session began with a brief welcome, introduction, and overview followed by a mind-body wellness exercise that focused on four primary elements: breathing, movement, imagery, and awareness. Students then participated in an ice-breaker activity in which percussive shakers were passed from individual to individual, the speed of transfer progressively accelerating to the point at which participants dropped the shakers and laughter ensued. The students were then given hand drums and given simple instructions on how to play these instruments in an expressive, non-performance-based manner designed to ensure an enjoyable musical experience. Halfway through the protocol, the students were asked to express themselves nonverbally by playing their drum in direct response to a series of questions developed by the research team with the hope of inspiring a sense of nurturing, support, and interpersonal respect. Each student was then given the option to discuss his or her nonverbal response. The researchers discovered that this particular intervention resulted in statistically significant improvements on multiple parameters associated with burnout, mood, and total mood disturbance. The researchers noted that although this particular RMM program would not necessarily influence every student to remain in a nursing program, the projected retention of just two individuals each year per program could result in substantially more nursing graduates and significant projected cost savings for both hospitals and universities.

In another study, "Recreational Music-Making: A Cost-Effective Group Interdisciplinary Strategy for Reducing Burnout and Improving Mood States in Long-Term Care Workers," Bittman, Bruhn, and colleagues sought to measure the potential economic impact of a six-session RMM protocol on burnout and mood dimensions as well as on total mood disturbance in an interdisciplinary group of long-term care workers.[8] The authors note the "spiral of instability" in the field of long-term healthcare workers brought about by an exodus of direct-care staff and the difficulties of recruiting and retaining qualified long-term healthcare workers. These industries typically have annual turnover rates of 40 percent and 100 percent respectively. In addition, U.S. populations of individuals over the ages of sixty-five and eighty-five are expected to steadily increase from 34.8 to 82 million, and 4.3 to 19.4 million, respectively, over the course of the next fifty years. Because of the combination of these two situations, there exists what is referred to as a "care gap" in the United States. Additional factors that lead to the undesirability of employment in the field of long-term healthcare include low wages, the challenge of caring for individuals with complex illnesses or dementia, heavy caseloads, issues related to death and dying, and the epidemic of crippling workplace injuries. Because of these challenges, companies that provide long-term care such as hospitals and nursing homes experience significant challenges to economic survival.

The researchers hypothesized that a six-session, cost-effective RMM protocol would result in diminished burnout and total mood disturbance in long-term care workers. In this experiment, a total of 125 subjects ranging in age from nineteen to seventy-eight were selected from among 375 employees of Westbury United Methodist

Retirement Community in Meadville, Pennsylvania. The project was presented to the workers as an employee-enrichment activity, with minimal information provided to participants in order to minimize potential expectation effects. Small groups met with a trained facilitator at a designated time each week for a total of six one-hour sessions. Facilitators, including a physician and a music teacher, followed the HealthRHYTHMS Group Empowerment Drumming Protocol and utilized a series of specially composed mind-body wellness exercises for the Clavinova. Instruments including hand drums, SoundShapes, a variety of auxiliary percussion instruments, and a Clavinova computerized electronic keyboard were chosen in order to allow individuals without prior music training to feel immediately successful. Each session began with a brief welcome followed by a five-minute mind-body wellness exercise played on the Clavinova. Subjects then participated in an ice-breaker activity identical to the one used in the previous study. Subjects selected a drum and tapped out simple rhythms after the facilitator presented a brief explanation of simple drumming techniques. Rather than attempting to learn complex rhythms, subjects then proceeded to play drums and percussion instruments together with Clavinova accompaniment of a familiar tune in order to ensure an enjoyable musical experience. Halfway through the protocol, subjects were asked to express themselves nonverbally while playing their drums in direct response to a series of questions developed by the authors of the study to inspire deep thought, contemplation, and mutual respect. Each subject was then given the option to discuss his or her nonverbal response, with individual comments typically evolving into highly charged group discussions moderated by the facilitator. Each session concluded by repeating the initial mind-body wellness Clavinova exercise and noting or discussing any physical or emotional changes experiences during and after the session.

After analyzing the data gathered from this experiment, the researchers discovered that the long-term healthcare workers involved in this study showed statistically significant improvements on multiple parameters associated with burnout, mood states, and total mood disturbance. The researchers point out the particular strengths and ease of implementation of group drumming, potentially because the defining philosophy of group-drumming intervention emphasizes support and personal or group expression, rather than mastery. Additionally, participants were simply asked to tap their drums to familiar tunes played on the Clavinova, which is a musical activity so accessible that it could most likely be executed by anyone, regardless of musical aptitude or previous training. The authors point out that significant cost savings could be attained by long-term care facilities if similar RMM protocols were implemented. Perhaps the power of RMM contributes to these cost savings by offering those in stressful fields opportunities to express themselves in music that is deeply personal, which serves as a motivator for developing and strengthening friendships in the workplace, as well as acceptance, support, and respect.

Musicians can informally attest to the fact that music is a transformative pursuit, that it literally changes them on deep physical and emotional levels. Some research undertaken in the field of RMM may prove that studying music can change humans on a measurable biological level. In their article "Recreational Music-Making Modulates Immunological Responses and Mood States in Older Adults," Masahiro Koyama and colleagues studied the questions of whether a RMM protocol could improve mood and modulate immunological responses in a direction opposite to that associated with chronic stress in older adults, and whether that protocol would affect older and younger participants in different ways. Two groups of volunteers, divided by whether they were over or under age sixty-five, underwent identical one-hour RMM interventions. Before and after these interventions data were collected using blood samples and mood state questionnaires. Data from twenty-seven volunteers from each age group were analyzed for various markers, including cytokine production levels, natural killer cell activity, plasma catecholamines, and number of T cells, T cell subsets, B cells, and natural killer cells. In the older group, significant increases in the number of lymphocytes, T cells, CD4+ T cells, and memory T cells and in production of interferon-Y and interleukin-6 were noted. In the younger group, no significant changes were recorded. In simpler terms, although mood states improved in both groups, the improvement in immunological profile and mood states in the older group, coupled with the low level of energy required to participate in the RMM protocol, was a significant vote for the effectiveness of RMM.[9]

In their article "Recreational Music Making Modulates the Human Stress Response: A Preliminary Individualized Gene Expression Strategy," Barry Bittman, Lee Berk, and colleagues measured the impact of an RMM program on gene markers related to stress. In subjects who performed the RMM activity, nineteen in forty-five gene markers for stress demonstrated reversal with significant correlations, in contrast to six in forty-five markers in a resting control group and zero in the ongoing stressor group. The researchers concluded from these results that RMM warrants additional consideration as a rational choice among the possible strategies for stress reduction.[10]

Another study, "Recreational Music-Making Alters Gene Expression Pathways in Patients with Coronary Heart Disease," by Barry Bittman and Daniel T. Croft Jr., describes the impact of an RMM protocol on patients with stress-related cardiovascular disease.[11] In this study, thirty-four participants with a history of ischemic heart disease were subjected to an acute time-limited stressor and then randomized to RMM or quiet reading for one hour. Peripheral blood gene expression using GeneChip Human Genome arrays were assessed at baseline, following stress, and after a relaxation session. The results of this study showed that relaxation by means of active engagement in RMM was more effective than quiet reading because participants in the RMM group had their gene expression altered more significantly. During relaxation, two pathways showed a significant change in expression in the group that participated in quiet reading, whereas twelve pathways that govern immune function and gene expression were modulated among RMM participants.

The research concerning the clinical impact of RMM on a number of physical and mental health conditions speaks quite strongly to the power of music study for a general population that may be hungry for improved quality of life. Whether in corporate environments that seek improved happiness and productivity from their employees, service-based industries that wish to positively impact and reward their workers, healthcare settings whose workers seek amelioration of the debilitating stress of their jobs, facilities with patients who face chronic illness or health problems, or in police and fire departments, whose members face strains and stresses in their jobs that may have a negative impact on their personal wellness, large swathes of the population stand to benefit from the advantages of RMM.

When considering these conditions and possibilities, the studio piano teacher stands to contribute significantly to the well-being of the community while also creating new entrepreneurial opportunities for his or her business. Possible avenues for exploration and lifelong learning include the National Piano

Foundation Recreational Music Making Teacher Scholarship, which is offered by the Music Teachers National Association thanks in part to a large grant from the NAMM. The National Piano Foundation offers a limited number of scholarships of between $500 and $750 to MTNA piano teachers who are interested in learning more about RMM. These scholarships must be used for travel, lodging, membership, fees, and other costs associated with attending the Pedagogy Saturday RMM Track. The MTNA Recreational Music Making Teaching Track enables piano teachers to learn about teaching RMM group classes with topics that include

- recreational group teaching within the independent studio
- conceptual teaching in the RMM classroom
- repertoire ideas for teachers of RMM
- RMM and the power of music to change lives in positive ways and
- networking for teachers of RMM.

Awardees of the National Piano Foundation Recreational Music Making Teacher Scholarship must sign an agreement stating that they demonstrate a commitment to developing a RMM group piano program in their community in partnership with a local piano retailer, music school, senior center, or other appropriate venue. Awardees must also submit quarterly updates about their group piano program in June, September, and December of the same year, with a final report due in March of the following year. These reports are to include teaching materials, number and age of students, appraisals of student progress, event programs, examples of promotional materials, and studio policies. Recipients of this scholarship must also work in partnership with the National Piano

Foundation to collect video testimonials from RMM teachers and their students, including the students' ages and progress, curricula information, and instrument sales and rentals resulting from their RMM classes.

The NAMM Foundation holds a yearly grant competition that is essentially a multimillion-dollar reinvestment in scientific research, advocacy, philanthropic giving, and public service programs related to making music. These grants are funded in part by donations from NAMM and its 9,900 member companies worldwide. Larger RMM organizations that reach broad segments of their community may consider applying for one of these large grants. In addition to these grants, NAMM provides resources online about the importance of RMM in the music-teaching landscape.

Another avenue is partnering with local organizations whose works deals in some way with quality-of-life issues. Depending on one's community, this list is potentially huge, and it might include hospitals, homeless shelters, foster care organizations, senior and assisted-living facilities, centers for at-risk teens, massage and acupuncture clinics, houses of worship, jails and prisons, psychologists' offices, community or civic centers, senior clubs or centers, social organizations offered by churches, gyms with a particular focus on wellness like the YMCA, after-school programs, and tutoring centers or youth detention facilities.

PRACTICAL IDEAS FOR RECREATIONAL MUSIC MAKING

Developing curricula for RMM may involve significant and detailed planning on the part of the piano teacher. The following are some ideas about how to easily reach the recreational music maker.

Find or develop age-appropriate resources for your RMM students. Elementary methods are designed specifically with the young child in mind. Although the musical content of these books may be effective and comprehensive for any level of beginner, learning from such a book can prove insulting for the adult beginning recreational music maker. Excellent adult methods are available from a number of publishers, as well as texts intended for college-level beginning group piano classes. Familiarize yourself with what is available so that your choices of materials honor the musical potential of your students while being age-appropriate in presentation.

Electronic keyboard technologies, while potentially excellent teaching tools for students of any level or age, may have particularly powerful uses for adult RMM students. Applications for such instruments as the Yamaha Clavinova provide ways for adult students to sequence their own compositions, play with tracks, and share their progress with their teacher. In addition, such students way may find the comparatively low cost of an electronic keyboard (and the minimal costs associated with maintenance) to be enticing.

The overarching goal of an adult recreational music maker must always be kept in mind during instruction. If the goal is to reduce stress, activities and curricula must be tailored to fit this aim, and periodic assessments of stress levels should be undertaken. These checks could involve monthly teaching evaluations to be filled out by the student, periodic wellness check-ins done in consultation with a mental health expert, or, even more simply, monthly lessons that take place not at the piano but at the local coffee shop. When the piano teacher recognizes his or her potential role as counselor, friend, and confidant, applying these skills becomes a natural fit when teaching students who are searching for larger meaning in their studies.

An idea that I have long believed in is that when we teach nontraditional students (like students with disabilities, adult beginners, or recreational music makers), we realize that music is "big" and not small, as we have been trained to believe based on the many hours we spend obsessing over details in cramped practice rooms. When a teacher sees the big picture of his or her impact in using this style of teaching, curriculum becomes easier to tailor to these exciting and impactful circumstances.

NOTES

1. Barry Bittman, Lee Berk, Mark Shannon, Muhammad Sharaf, Jim Westengard, Karl J. Guegler, and David W. Ruff, "Recreational Music-Making Modulates the Human Stress Response: A Preliminary Individualized Gene Expression Strategy," *Medical Science Monitor* 11, no. 2 (2005): BR31–BR40.
2. Brenda Dillon, "The Joys of Making: Observations Regarding Recreational Music Making," *American Music Teacher* 59, no. 2 (2009): 20–23.
3. Brian Chung and Brenda Dillon, "Piano Teaching—Traditional or Recreational? What's the Difference?" *American Music Teacher* 58, no. 2 (2008): 46–47.
4. Ibid.
5. Quoted in Rebecca Johnson, "Take Two Lessons and Call Me in the Morning," *Clavier Companion* 18, no. 2 (2007): 32.
6. Brenda Dillon, "Student-Centered Outcomes," *Clavier Companion* 18, no. 3 (2007): 32–35.
7. Barry Bittman et al., "Recreational Music-Making: An Integrative Group Intervention for Reducing Burnout and Improving Mood States in First-Year Associate Degree Nursing Students; Insights and Economic Impact," *International Journal of Nursing Education Scholarship* 1, no. 1 (2005): 1044.
8. Barry Bittman, Karl T. Bruhn, Christine Stevens, James Westengard, and Paul O. Umbach, "Recreational Music-Making: A Cost-Effective Group Interdisciplinary Strategy for Reducing Burnout and Improving Mood States in Long-Term Care Workers," *Advances in Mind-Body Medicine* 19, nos. 3–4 (2003): 4–15.
9. Masahiro Koyama et al., "Recreational music-making modulates immunological responses and mood states in older adults." *Journal of Medical and Dental Sciences* 56, no. 2 (2009): 79.

10. Bittman, Berk, Shannon, Sharaf, Westengard, Guegler, and Ruff, "Recreational Music-Making."
11. Barry Bittman, Daniel T. Croft Jr, Jeannie Brinker, Ryan van Laar, Marina N. Vernalis, and Darrell L. Ellsworth. "Recreational Music-Making Alters Gene Expression Pathways in Patients with Coronary Heart Disease." *Medical Science Monitor: International Medical Journal of Experimental and Clinical Research* 19 (2013): 139.

Chapter 5

Working with Pianists with Depression

Trevor is a thirteen-year-old boy in eighth grade from an intact, seemingly happy family, and he has been a student in your piano studio since the age of five. You consider Trevor to be bright, musical, creative, respectful, and confident. He has placed highly in competitions and even won a few, has performed with self-assurance in your studio recitals, and has received consistently high marks in the local Student Achievement Music Theory Exams year after year. Over the past three months, you have noticed that Trevor has not been prepared for his lessons and has clearly not been practicing enough or at all. In his lessons Trevor seems inattentive and shows little interest in activities you have planned. He is not particularly disruptive or rude but seems to want to avoid interacting with other students in your studio. When you ask him why he has not been practicing, he says things like, "I don't know. It's not that important. No one cares if I can play the piano anyway." You hear from Trevor's parents that he occasionally becomes irritable or angry when asked to do his chores and homework. Trevor's parents occasionally describe him as lazy and unmotivated, and at times they seem as if they have given up on trying to help him become motivated to work. You are puzzled by what seems like a different Trevor, but the motivating tactics you have used before are not working.

The story outlined above is based on a student I have worked with and may reflect the characteristics of some children, pre-teens, and teenagers who are suffering from depression. Depressed students who are not formally recognized as such may be viewed by teachers, parents, and peers as lazy and may not respond to traditional methods of discipline and encouragement. It's important for a teacher to understand that depressed children are not trying to be defiant or uncooperative but, rather, they simply cannot summon the personal emotional resources to perform to their maximum potential. A depressed child may rationalize in ways that are not productive, using thoughts like "I performed poorly at the recital because I am stupid," rather than "I performed poorly because I didn't practice enough." A depressed child may also think in particularly uncompromising terms, for example, "I am terrible at everything that I do" or "I just don't see the point in trying," rather than "I am good at doing some things and not very good at doing other things," or "I understand that if I work hard, I will become better." It is important for music teachers to understand that they will most likely work with depressed students and to know how to spot and work with them in order to adequately reach these students in an impactful way.

RECOGNIZING DEPRESSION

In the piano studio, depressed students may appear to be unmotivated and uncaring about their musical work when they are actually just unable to perform to their highest potential. Young people experience a number of behavioral disturbances that contribute to the development of a depressive disorder, including interpersonal disorders, an inability to use social skills, and a lack of participation in recreational and extracurricular activities.[1] Depressed students may have trouble sustaining attention, maintaining an effective and appropriate level of effort, and keeping up meaningful social relationships. If left untreated, depression has the ability to mushroom into more serious academic and social difficulties, dangerous substance abuse, general risk-taking behavior, and suicidal ideation and actions.[2] These behaviors may continue into adulthood if a child's depression is not treated in an effective way. While students with depression should receive counseling or therapy from a licensed expert, music teachers can play a mentoring role in collaboration with parents, schoolteachers, school psychologists, and school administrators by simply knowing what to look for and how to be most helpful.

HOW COMMON IS DEPRESSION IN CHILDREN?

Depression, a fairly common and yet widely unrecognized condition of childhood and adolescence, is frequently mistaken for a problem with behavior and motivation. It is estimated that up to 10 percent of students experience depression of a nature serious enough to require professional intervention and that up to 20 percent of all adults will have a depressive disorder at some time in their lives.[3] Adolescent girls and women are statistically twice as likely to develop depression as are adolescent boys and men. Yet in pre-adolescent girls and pre-adolescent boys there is no difference in the frequency of depression. These statistics indicate that in a piano studio of twenty students, as many as two students are likely to have mild to serious depression. It is vital that the piano teacher recognize that this is possible and that these students need a particular kind of care in order to thrive.

Anyone who has adolescent children or who has worked with adolescents understands that, particularly at this age, mood swings, feelings of frustration, and arguments with friends, parents, and even teachers are common occurrences. In a nondepressed student these mood swings do not typically last long and usually don't affect the student's academic and extra-curricular performance. Depression, however, is a much more serious condition in which an individual constantly feels down, blue, or sad. It can be easy for a nondepressed person to feel that a student with depression must simply "snap out of it," but it is critical to understand that a depressed student is not able to simply will himself or herself out of a state of depression.

Behavior that may be a sign of depression may include a depressed feeling for an extended period of time. Depressed students may lose interest or pleasure in almost all of the activities that they typically enjoy doing, even those in which they feel they excel. Even the most talented and successful young piano students may lose almost all interest in the very activity that sets them apart. Depressed students may occasionally be particularly angry, experience significant changes in appetite, and lose or gain an unusual amount of weight in a short period of time. Depressed students may experience a drastic change in their sleeping patterns, sleeping either much more or much less than usual. They often experience drastically decreased energy and may take part in a noticeably smaller amount of physical activity and exercise. They may exhibit feelings of guilt and worthlessness and may have significant difficulties thinking, concentrating, and remembering. Depressed students may have a hard time making even minor decisions and may have particularly negative thoughts about themselves, the world around them, and their future. Seriously depressed students may harbor thoughts of suicide and may even plan or attempt to die. Depressed students may feel listless and tired or may have few or no feelings at all. Students with depression may blame themselves for things that are not at all their fault and may find themselves unattractive. Not all depressed children will show all of these signs, but several of these signs together in a student may indicate that he or she is battling depression.[4]

SUICIDE

The greatest risk associated with depression is suicide. Although it is well beyond the piano teacher's skill set to act as a preventer of suicide, the outside possibility that depression may have this tragic result should be enough for the piano teacher to understand its warning signs and potential causes. A small percentage of depressed students show serious thoughts of planning or attempting suicide, but the vast majority of students with depression do not attempt the act. Predicting suicide is extraordinarily challenging because of its low frequency and because it is basically impossible to create a profile of those who have gone through with the act. Thoughts of suicide tend to occur more when people begin to feel that nothing will help improve their situation. Behaviors that indicate that an individual is having serious thoughts of suicidal planning may include giving away personal or prized belongings, taking care of personal matters such as repaying debts, or completing long-held personal challenges. People with suicidal ideation may suddenly visit family members whom they have not seen in a while and talk about how they would like to be remembered after they die. If you suspect that any of your students are considering suicide, do not be afraid to ask them about the risk of danger to themselves or others. It's a myth that one can "plant the idea" in a depressed person's head by asking. Typically, depressed students are relieved to know that you are taking them seriously and that the idea of suicide is out in the open for discussion. If a student isn't thinking of suicide he or she often is quick to reassure you of this fact, which can help you relax about the need for emergency intervention and help you feel it is safe for the student to be alone. If it is clear that a student of yours is having serious suicidal thoughts and feelings, a Suicide Lethality Assessment can help you evaluate how involved and detailed that suicidal thinking is and how lethal his or her proposed method is. Questions you might ask a person whom you believe is a risk for suicide include the following:

- Do you have a plan or method?
- Do you have access to the means of [carrying out] your plan?
- Do you have a time or event in mind that might trigger your suicide?
- Do you truly intend to act on your ideas?
- Are you feeling hopeless and/or helpless?
- Are you suffering from significant depression or experiencing a major loss in your life?
- When you think of committing suicide, does it get to a point where you think of how you might go through with the act?
- Is the method of suicide available to you (does the person have access to pills or the gun)?
- Do you feel that you will truly act on the plan in your head?
- Do you feel helpless about things in your life changing for the better?
- What, so far, has kept you from acting on your suicidal thinking?

- What supports do you have?
- What are you willing to do if you feel more suicidal and think you might act on it?
- Do you think that you might be able to call a crisis line if your thinking became more dangerous and you might act on it?[5]

Based on the student's responses to these questions, you as the teacher might consider making a referral to a trained psychologist or health professional or to call 911. Some students in this situation might be immediately receptive to this idea, but others will need considerable reassurance in order to feel safe about proceeding to a mental health professional. It can be helpful to normalize the idea of a referral by saying something like, "There are thousands of teenagers in your situation every year. Many of them are dealing with issues exactly like yours." You also can plant an idea in a potentially suicidal student's mind to get him or her to consider seeking professional help. The following statement might serve such a purpose: "You seem reluctant to seek professional help now, and it seems like you feel confident that your mental situation will improve. I want to give you some information about someone you might be able to see who could offer you some excellent help. You can also talk to me about this again if you change your mind and want to seek professional help."

If the threat to a student seems minimal, you may want to simply suggest counseling services. If you fear that a student might not follow through with seeking the help of a professional, you may want to offer to schedule an appointment for him or her. If you are especially concerned for a student, you might want to physically escort him or her to a counseling center or hospital emergency room to make sure that the proper intervention happens, or, if the student is a minor, call 911 and notify his or her parents. If a student replies yes to questions about suicide, and if the response indicates that the action might be imminent, do not leave this person alone, and call for emergency medical help immediately.

WHAT CAUSES DEPRESSION?

Depression is a complex syndrome with a large matrix of causes. People who have a greater than normal likelihood of developing depression include those who have close relatives with depression, those who live in a highly stressful situation, and those who have lived through an intensely traumatic event.[6] Depression may be a long-term condition or it may be of recent onset, as is often the case with trauma. Long-term depression is significantly more difficult to treat and almost always requires professional help. Almost all depression experts agree that it is caused by fundamental changes in the chemistry of neurotransmitters in the brain.[7]

Some studies indicate that children who believe that others do not view them as competent are more likely to develop depression.[8] This particular view has obvious implications for the private music teacher, namely, that if the teacher does not let a student know that he or she is musically capable, there may be a greater risk for the student to develop depression. In addition, because high-achieving applied music studios can be stressful places for children who are not musically competent or successful, these students may be at an increased risk for developing depression. Studies show that students who have not been successful at school relate feelings of sadness and depression because they do not perform well.[9]

Depression is occasionally associated with other conditions that afflict children. Approximately 50 percent of children with depression also have problems with anxiety.[10] Depression and anxiety have many similar symptoms, making it difficult for specialists to develop a primary syndrome. Depression also co-occurs with Attention Deficit Hyperactivity Disorder, Oppositional Defiant Disorder, Conduct Disorder, and substance abuse problems in up to 79 percent of cases.[11] It is critical for the music teacher to understand that students who have problems that might be described as "acting out" may also be clinically depressed. Patience and understanding are perhaps the most important traits for the successful mentoring piano teacher to have. Without a knowledge of the symptoms and the impact of a condition such as depression, a music teacher may not only overlook the root cause of a student's worsening performance but may also exacerbate its negative consequences.

EFFECTIVE AND APPROPRIATE TEACHER INTERVENTIONS

Depression is a tremendously complicated human condition, especially when it co-occurs with other emotional and behavioral problems. Many times, family problems aggravate symptoms of depression and may even be root causes, making intervention on the part of a teacher even more difficult. Fortunately, with proper intervention, most children with depression can overcome the syndrome and lead happy and productive adult lives. Professional treatment is obviously beyond what is expected of a music teacher. Yet there are many things that teachers and mentors can do to assist the depressed student.

Develop a sincere and caring relationship. Communicate frequently with the depressed student and try to develop a collaborative relationship. Do not be afraid to talk with the student openly about his or her condition. Many times, depressed students are seeking someone who cares about them, someone who may assist with their feelings. Do not give up on students with depression. Show them that they have worth, show them that they are intelligent, and show them that their musical contribution to the world is worthwhile and vital.

Harness positivity. Do not use punishment, disparagement, sarcasm, or negative feedback techniques with a student with depression. These tactics are likely to reinforce feelings of incompetence and low self-esteem in the depressed student.

Understand that the student does not choose to be depressed. Depressed students do not have the personal resources to do their best work. Just as a student with a reading disability would not be expected to read at grade level, students with depression should not be expected to perform at the same level as their nondepressed peers. A depressed music student needs to receive extra support, therefore.

Make adjustments or accommodations in weekly musical assignments. This approach should not mean that your expectations of a depressed student should be lowered; however, a depressed student should be given more time to finish pieces, assignments should be broken into smaller pieces, and extra help should be offered. For example, you can introduce new repertoire extensively during a lesson, consider setting up extra "practice" lessons in order to enable a sense of accomplishment, pride, and worth in the depressed student, and consider pairing such a student with an older and more veteran member of the studio who may be particularly caring and willing to assist.

Foster success. Arrange performance experiences for students with depression so that they receive external recognition for their good efforts, in the hope that it helps instill an internal mechanism of positive feedback. Take it upon yourself to ensure that a student with depression is beyond prepared for studio recitals, festivals, and competitions. Personally support them on the days of big performance events, taking care to build success on success in a safe and low-risk way. Be sure that all of your students feel that they are socially accepted within your studio.

Seek help from experts. Consult with psychologists, counselors, or social workers within your student's orbit, whether at school or privately consulted. Every student is an individual and should receive your individual attention. This may require hours outside of your lesson time with a depressed student, but understand that your impact on a such a student is much larger than that of a music instructor.[12]

NOTES

1. Kevin D. Stark, Jennifer Hargrave, Brooke Hersh, Michelle Greenberg, Jenny Herren, and Melissa Fisher, "Treatment of Childhood Depression," in *Handbook of Depression in Children and Adolescents,* edited by John R. Z. Abela and Benjamin L. Hankin, 224–249 (New York: Guilford, 2008).
2. William M. Reynolds and Hugh F. Johnston, eds., *Handbook of Depression in Children and Adolescents.* (Berlin: Springer Science and Business Media, 2013).
3. Larry S. Goldman, Nancy H. Nielsen, and Hunter C. Champion, "Awareness, Diagnosis, and Treatment of Depression," *Journal of General Internal Medicine* 14, no. 9 (1999): 569–580.
4. Ronald C. Kessler, Shelli Avenevoli, and Kathleen Ries Merikangas, "Mood Disorders in Children and Adolescents: An Epidemiologic Perspective," *Biological Psychiatry* 49, no. 12 (2001): 1002–1014.
5. Nilamadhab Kar, Mohanram Arun, Manoj K. Mohanty, and Binaya K. Bastia, "Scale for Assessment of Lethality of Suicide Attempt," *Indian Journal of Psychiatry* 56, no. 4 (2014): 337–343.
6. Michael Fendrich, Virginia Warner, and Myrna M. Weissman, "Family Risk Factors, Parental Depression, and Psychopathology in Offspring," *Developmental Psychology* 26, no. 1 (1990): 40–50.
7. Matthew S. Lebowitz, Woo-kyoung Ahn, and Susan Nolen-Hoeksema, "Fixable or Fate? Perceptions of the Biology of Depression." *Journal of Consulting and Clinical Psychology* 81, no. 3 (2013): 518–527.

8. Laurence Steinberg, "We Know Some Things: Parent–Adolescent Relationships in Retrospect and Prospect," *Journal of Research on Adolescence* 11, no. 1 (2001): 1–19.
9. Gwen M. Glew, Ming-yu Fan, Wayne Katon, Frederick P. Rivara, and Mary A. Kernic, "Bullying, Psychosocial Adjustment, and Academic Performance in Elementary School," *Archives of Pediatrics and Adolescent Medicine* 159, no. 11 (2005): 1026–1031.
10. Annette M. La Greca and Hannah Moore Harrison, "Adolescent Peer Relations, Friendships, and Romantic Relationships: Do They Predict Social Anxiety and Depression?" *Journal of Clinical Child and Adolescent Psychology* 34, no. 1 (2005): 49–61.
11. E. Jane Costello, Sarah Mustillo, Alaattin Erkanli, Gordon Keeler, and Adrian Angold, "Prevalence and Development of Psychiatric Disorders in Childhood and Adolescence," *Archives of General Psychiatry* 60, no. 8 (2003): 837–844.
12. Ralph E. Cash, "When It Hurts to Be a Teenager," *Principal Leadership* 4, no. 2 (2003): 11–15.

Chapter 6

Working with Pianists with High-Functioning Autism

High-functioning autism is a disorder on the autism spectrum that is distinguished by difficulties in social interaction and nonverbal communication, along with restricted and sometimes repetitive patterns of behavior and interests. Generally, those with what used to be called Asperger syndrome have normal or near-normal linguistic and cognitive development. Children with learning disabilities such as high-functioning autism (HFA) in the modern piano studio pose an exciting challenge to music teachers, requiring them to use a variety of teaching strategies in order to reach these students.

In a study of public school teachers by V. Cumine, J. Leach, and Gill Stevenson,[1] a majority of teachers felt that they had not received the proper training to instruct children with HFA. My informal polls of piano teachers tell me that the same feelings exist among most piano teachers. Teachers should aim to expand their repertoire of research-based strategies for teaching students with HFA in order to serve these exceptional students with joy and effectiveness.

RESEARCH IN AUTISM INSTRUCTION

The body of research concerning the broad spectrum of autism is significantly larger than that for HFA specifically. Although HFA and more severe autism differ with regard to early cognitive development and language acquisition, similarities do exist. Because of these similarities, some of the teaching strategies put forth in general autism research are applicable to working with students with HFA.

The behaviorist theory, or "behaviorism," is an approach to psychology that is primarily concerned with the observable and measurable aspects of human behavior while emphasizing changes in behavior that result from stimulus-response associations made by the learner.[2] With regard to HFA, "maladaptive behavior is viewed as essentially the result of (1) a failure to learn necessary adaptive behaviors or competencies, such as how to establish satisfying personal relationships, and/or (2) the learning of ineffective or maladaptive responses."[3] The first of these describes students with HFA very well. Such learners sometimes do not detect social cues such as a facial expression meant to convey frustration. Missing nonverbal social cues can result in not learning the lesson associated with a given experience.

Although individuals on the autism spectrum sometimes have difficulty determining another person's emotions and desires, they are often very well aware of their own. This can be very useful in the context of a music lesson if an instructor takes the time to determine what is pleasing to a student. For example, if a student with HFA finds particular pleasure in learning to play the music from *Star Wars*, a teacher should take notice and use this desired activity as reinforcement for another task (for example, the practicing of scales).

DESIGNING TEACHING STRATEGIES BASED ON RESEARCH

Characteristics of HFA often are masked by above-average IQ scores. Because of this, teachers may presume that a student is capable of more than is being produced. A music teacher who does not understand the specific needs of an AS student may not as readily search for strategies for reaching that student. In addition, pupils with HFA frequently find social situations distracting and overwhelming. Group music instruction, chamber music, and work in large ensembles may be so challenging for such students that learning goals may be lost completely. Music teachers should harness the advantages of one-on-one applied music instruction. Whereas public education involves consistent socialization with group assignments, passing periods, lunch breaks, and recess, the private, controlled nature of a music lesson can be a comfortable and native environment for a student with HFA.

As Pat Romanowski Bashe and Linda Kirby report, if asked to design an environment specifically geared to stress a person with High Functioning Autism Syndrome, you would probably come up with something that looked a lot like a school. You would want an overwhelming number of peers; periods of tightly structured time alternating with periods lacking any structure; regular helpings of irritating noise from bells, schoolmates, band practice, alarms, and crowded, cavernous spaces; countless distractions; a dozen or so daily transitions with a few surprises thrown in now and then; and finally, the piece de resistance: regularly scheduled tours into what can only be described as socialization hell (a.k.a. recess, lunch, gym, and the bus ride to and from school). It's a wonder that so many children with AS manage to do so well.[4]

In many ways the private music lesson is exactly the opposite of the school scenario described by these researchers: More often than not, no peers are present, lesson time and content can be much more flexible than in a school, potentially irritating ambient noise can be limited and controlled, and a sense of calm can be created and supported by a caring teacher in an intentional way.

Karen Williams describes the great importance of minimizing stress and worry in a student with HFA and the educational advantages of such an approach.[5] Williams emphasizes that minimizing transitions and ensuring a predictable environment can help such a student feel more comfortable while learning. She also recommends that the student be thoroughly prepared in advance of changes in educational routines so that a preoccupation with what will come next will not occur. Most of our music students, on and off the autism spectrum, experience anxiety and nervousness with regard to performances and competitions. These feelings may be amplified in students with HFA. Their experience will be improved if these events are predictable, calm, well-run, and free of last-minute changes.

Many piano students successfully switch teachers at some point in the course of their education, but such changes can be particularly disruptive and stressful for a student with HFA. Diane Adreon and Jennifer Stella[6] address these types of transitions in the public school curriculum and advocate "transition-planning meetings," which allow the previous instructor to educate the incoming teacher about strategies that have worked for an individual with high-functioning autism. In addition, the researchers suggest allowing the student to have extra time to become familiar with a new learning environment. It would benefit such a student greatly if teachers would work in tandem when transferring teaching responsibilities. When geography does not permit, the use of videoconferencing software such as Skype or FaceTime could provide an opportunity for a transition-planning meeting.

APPLIED BEHAVIOR ANALYSIS AND DISCRETE TRIAL TRAINING

Applied behavior analysis and discrete trial training (ABA/DTT) is a teaching technique that is highly effective with students on the autism spectrum. Discrete trial training is the science of breaking down learning into small steps that build on each other, leading eventually to the understanding of an overall concept.[7] Applying the principles of ABA/DTT helps a student focus on small pieces of information, creating a better opportunity to complete an assignment. This logical process can help a student sort through the many confusing bits of stimulation received throughout the day. A teacher can apply discrete trial training to music instruction through careful lesson planning, both during an individual lesson and over the course of a set of lessons. For example, working together with a student on the right hand only through the end of the exposition would be a much more effective small step than sending the student home to practice the entirety of a sonatina movement on his or her own.

WRITING EXERCISE: Write a lesson plan for a six-year-old beginning student based on the breaking down of the material into small assignments suggested by ABA/DTT. Create this assignment using a Primer Level method book from a major series.

TEACCH METHOD

A widely used approach to autism education is the Treatment and Education of Autistic and related Communication-handicapped Children program, commonly known as the TEACCH method. Sally Ozonoff, Geraldine Dawson, and James C. McPartland describe this method as a way to build on the particular memory strengths of a child with HFA.[8] Many students with ASD have the ability to remember large quantities of information about subjects that pique their interest. For example, a child with HFA may be fascinated with jetliners and will offer as much information on the subject as would an aeronautical engineer. The four main elements of TEACCH are as follows:

1. an intentionally structured classroom
2. a visual schedule of the day's activities (visual instructions and schedules help reduce insecurity and lessen stress, which may detract to learning)
3. an explanation of the type and length of the schoolwork expected
4. instructions presented both visually and verbally

These concepts provide what the researchers describe as "scaffolding" for the AS student; that is, new learning occurs with a solid support structure based on organization and visual representations.

WRITING EXERCISE: Create a visual schedule of the activities planned for a lesson with a fourth-year intermediate eleven-year-old with HFA based on principle #2 of the TEACHH method.

WINGS MENTOR PROGRAM

The Wings Mentor Program is designed to improve students' self-confidence, positively change other student's perceptions of them, and improve their motivation to learn. According to Betty Shevitz and colleagues, "these are the students who rarely have homework completed, or if done, cannot find it. They are light years ahead in math, but reading below grade level. These same students may not only be able to program the computer, but they may be able to take it apart completely and put it back together again. Ask them about the Civil War, DNA cloning, lasers, or ancient civilizations and you might be bombarded with information and unique insights. Ask them to write about the same topic and they may produce little or nothing."[9]

The Wings Mentor Program addresses this problem by having a student work directly with a mentor (an obvious natural strength of the one-on-one nature of the music lesson). The mentor determines a topic that the student may struggle with, while the student chooses an area of study that preoccupies him or her. These topics are studied with the mentor for a period of eight weeks, at the end of which students share their projects at a "show-off night."

The applications of the Wings Mentor Program for music study are numerous. A high-functioning autistic preoccupied with improvisation but less enthusiastic about scales and arpeggios may improve in technical studies should his or her preoccupation with improvisation be cultivated, for example. In addition, show-off night activities could be integrated into studio recitals or could replace competitions and festivals in order to take advantage of the strengths of our AS students. Moreover, opportunities for AS students to exhibit their knowledge in a favorite field may provide learning opportunities for their studio colleagues, as well as opportunities to improve respect among peers.

SCOPE AND SEQUENCE

Students with HFA are often unable to generalize the skills that they learn. For example, when taught a scale fingering, such students may not understand that the same fingering could be used for fragments of the same scale in the sonatina that they are learning. Brenda Smith Myles and Richard L. Simpson suggest that a mode of instruction called "scope and sequence" may be useful in helping students generalize concepts.[10] Scope and sequence is defined by the authors as teaching students about specifics and basics before expecting them to learn generalized rules. In musical instruction, connecting the dots between the learning of a concept in the abstract (scale fingerings) and the application (scale fingerings in a piece of repertoire) is an example of scope-and-sequence learning. An inability to generalize can also pose problems in basic tasks that our students are expected to do. For example, a student with HFA may simply not begin playing in a competition setting if not told to do so. Research concerning scope and sequence suggests that instructors give all the steps necessary to complete a task or assignment rather than assuming that a high-functioning autistic will naturally know what comes next. For example, a competition judge could ask the student to (1) make himself or herself comfortable at the piano, (2) adjust the bench if desired, (3) try out the instrument, and (4) begin playing when ready.

OTHER CONSIDERATIONS FOR WORKING WITH STUDENTS ON THE AUTISM SPECTRUM

Research concerning music education indicates that children on the autism spectrum do not imitate the actions of others with the same understanding and mastery as their typically developing classmates. Imitation and rote teaching are tried-and-true methods of teaching music to students of varying levels. Motor impairments and the inability to transfer visual information to a psychomotor response generally pose significant difficulties for students with an autism spectrum disorder. Because children learn new skills by mimicking others, imitative behaviors are "an important focus of early intervention programs for children with autism."[11] Because autism is a disorder that occurs on a spectrum, no two children respond to pedagogical initiatives in the same way. It is critical, therefore, that teachers be flexible in developing pedagogies that meet the needs of the individual. Most important, music teachers should approach tasks involving imitation with patience, knowing that learning by imitation can be more difficult for children on the autism spectrum than for their typically developing studio mates.

Tiffany Field, Jacqueline Nadel, and Shauna Ezell have observed that children on the autism spectrum responded positively to playful adults, especially if the adults imitate the children's behaviors.[12] These researchers noted that such children looked at, touched, and moved toward an adult stranger who imitated their actions. Moreover, children involved in this research study showed more social behaviors with strangers who imitated their actions than they exhibited when interacting with their own parents. In order to apply these observations to piano teaching, it is important for the teacher to understand that children on the autism spectrum will display more social behaviors with piano teachers who imitate their actions. This mode of teaching represents a significant shift from the modes of imitation and rote teaching that we typically rely on, modes in which the child remembers the initial presentation of the adult. In a way, this could be considered a student-centered imitation in which the adult follows the child.

One of the useful aspects of AS research is its potential application to students both on and off the autism spectrum. Most important, it reminds us of the fact that each of our students is an individual with unique learning strengths and struggles. It is essential that music teachers understand what HFA is and take the time to educate themselves about teaching strategies for these students.

CENTERS OF RESEARCH AND PRACTICE FOR TEACHING PIANISTS WITH AUTISM SPECTRUM DISORDERS

The National Conference on Keyboard Pedagogy's Committee for Teaching Students with Special Needs is comprised of individuals who have undertaken significant initiatives for teaching students with autism that involve research, outreach, and teacher training (including the author of this book). Three of these initiatives are listed below.

The Carolina LifeSong Initiative, http://www.sc.edu/study/colleges_schools/music/study/performance_areas/keyboard/pianopedagogy/carolina_lifesong_initiative.php, headed by Scott Price, serves students with special needs and includes them in activities in which they may excel. The initiative provides piano instruction and music experiences for people with autism, ADD/ADHD, developmental delays, Down syndrome, and hearing and visual impairments.

Beethoven's Buddies, http://www.bethbauerpiano.com/beethoven-s-buddies.html, is the brainchild of Wheaton College faculty member Beth Bauer. Beethoven's Buddies is an innovative piano program for students with special needs of all kinds, including autism, fragile X, ADD/ADHD, Down syndrome, visual impairment, auditory and visual processing disorders, and dyslexia.

Celebrating the Spectrum: A Festival of Music and Life, http://www.music.msu.edu/spectrum, created by Derek Kealii Polischuk. A week-long festival held every July, Celebrating the Spectrum is held at the College of Music at Michigan State University. The festival is designed to give qualified advanced pre-college students on the autism spectrum a preview of a life in music. The student's daily schedule reflects the life of a music major in a university or conservatory setting and culminates in two live performances. All students perform daily in master classes conducted by College of Music piano faculty members Deborah Moriarty and Derek Kealii Polischuk. Classes are devoted to solo repertoire as well as piano four-hand repertoire.

NOTES

1. Val Cumine, Julia Dunlop, and Gill Stevenson, *Asperger Dyndrome: A Practical Guide for Teachers* (London: Routledge, 2010).
2. Stanford Encyclopedia of Philosophy, s.v. "Behaviorism." Accessed July 9, 2018. https://plato.stanford.edu/entries/behaviorism/.
3. J. Butcher, S. Mineka, and J. Hooley, *Abnormal Psychology* (Boston: Pearson Education, 2004).
4. Patricia Romanowski Bashe and Barbara L. Kirby, *The Oasis Guide to Asperger Syndrome: Advice, Support, Insight, and Inspiration* (New York: Crown Publishers, 2005).
5. Karen Williams, "Understanding the Student with Asperger Syndrome: Guidelines for Teachers," *Intervention in School and Clinic* 36, no. 5 (2001): 287–292.
6. Diane Adreon and Jennifer Stella, "Transition to Middle and High School: Increasing the Success of Students with Asperger Syndrome," *Intervention in School and Clinic* 36, no. 5 (2001): 266–271.
7. Dorothea C. Lerman, Brian A. Iwata, and Gregory P. Hanley, "Applied Behavior Analysis." In *APA Handbook of Behavior Analysis*, 81–104 (Washington DC: American Psychological Association, 2013).

8. Sally Ozonoff, Geraldine Dawson, and James C. McPartland, *A Parent's Guide to Asperger Syndrome and High-Functioning Autism: How to Meet the Challenges and Help Your Child Thrive* (New York: Guilford, 2002).
9. Betty Shevitz, Rich Weinfeld, Sue Jeweler, and Linda Barnes-Robinson, "Mentoring Empowers Gifted/Learning Disabled Students to Soar!" *Roeper Review* 26, no. 1 (2003): 37–40.
10. Brenda Smith Myles and Richard L. Simpson, "Understanding the Hidden Curriculum: An Essential Social Skill for Children and Youth with Asperger Syndrome," *Intervention in School and Clinic* 36, no. 5 (2001): 279–286.
11. Brooke Ingersoll and Laura Schreibman, "Teaching Reciprocal Imitation Skills to Young Children with Autism Using a Naturalistic Behavioral Approach: Effects on Language, Pretend Play, and Joint Attention," *Journal of Autism and Developmental Disorders* 36, no. 4 (2006): 487–505.
12. Tiffany Field, Jacqueline Nadel, and Shauna Ezell, "Imitation Therapy for Young Children with Autism." In *Autism Spectrum Disorders: From Genes to Environment*, edited by Tim Williams, 287–298 (N.p.: InTech, 2011).

Chapter 7

Working with Pianists with Attention Deficit Hyperactivity Disorder

Attention deficit hyperactivity disorder, or ADHD, is a common childhood disorder that piano teachers are likely to encounter during their career. This disorder can continue through adolescence and into adulthood. Common symptoms of ADHD may include extreme difficulty maintaining focus, paying attention, and regulating emotions and behavior, as well as hyperactivity.[1]

Attention deficit hyperactivity disorder is a fairly large class of disorders that has three main subcategories:

- **Predominantly hyperactive-impulsive.** Most symptoms are in the area of hyperactivity-impulsivity. Within this subcategory, fewer than six symptoms of inattention exist, although inattention may still be present on some level.
- **Predominantly inattentive.** Most symptoms are in the area of inattention. Within this subcategory, fewer than six symptoms of impulsivity are present, although hyperactivity-impulsivity may still occur on some level. Children within this subtype typically are less likely to have difficulties getting

along with other children and are able to sit quietly. Despite appearances, however, children who are predominantly inattentive may not be paying attention to the task they seem to be doing. Their disorder may be overlooked because parents and teachers may find it difficult to realize that a child has ADHD.

- **Combined hyperactive-impulsive and inattentive.** Six or more symptoms are in the inattention category and six or more symptoms are in the hyperactivity-impulsivity category. Most children with ADHD fall within this combined type of diagnosis.[2]

POSSIBLE CAUSES OF ADHD

Scientists are not sure what causes ADHD, although a large number of studies suggest that genetics plays a formidable role. Like many illnesses, attention deficit hyperactivity disorder likely results from a combination of factors, including genetics, environment, brain injuries, nutrition, and upbringing.

Studies of twins have shown that ADHD often runs in families.[3] Researchers are currently looking at several genes that may make people more likely to develop this illness. Children with ADHD who carry a particular version of a certain genetic line have thinner brain tissue in the cerebral cortex, the area of the brain associated with attention.[4] This particular study showed that this difference in brain thickness was not permanent, and as children with this gene became adults, the brain in these areas typically developed to a normal level of thickness. Accordingly, their ADHD symptoms also improved with time.

With regard to environment, studies have suggested a potential link between cigarette smoking and alcohol use during pregnancy and attention deficit hyperactivity disorder in children.[5] Moreover, preschoolers who are exposed to high levels of lead, sometimes found in paint and plumbing fixtures in old buildings, may have a higher risk of developing ADHD.[6] Children who have suffered a brain injury may show behaviors similar to those present with ADHD.[7] That being said, only a small percentage of children with ADHD have suffered a traumatic brain injury.

The idea that consuming large amounts of refined sugar causes ADHD is popular, but research largely discounts this premise. In one study, researchers gave children foods containing sugar or a sugar substitute every other day. The children who received sugar showed no difference in behavior or ability to learn than those who received the sugar substitute.[8] In another study, children who were described as "sugar-sensitive" by their mothers were given the sugar substitute aspartame. Although all of the children in this study received aspartame, half of their mothers were told that their children were given sugar, and the other half were told that their children were given aspartame. The mothers who thought their children had received sugar rated them more hyperactive than the children who received aspartame and were more critical of their behavior.[9]

Recent research has indicated a possible link between consumption of certain food additives, in particular artificial colors or preservatives, and an increase in hyperactivity.[10] More research is needed to confirm the findings and to learn more about how food additives affect hyperactivity.

SYMPTOMS OF ADHD

The telltale signs of ADHD are inattention, hyperactivity, and impulsivity. Of course, all young children are inattentive, hyperactive, and impulsive to some degree. But children with ADHD exhibit these behaviors with more severity and frequency. A child must have symptoms for six or more months and have a greater degree of severity than other children of the same age to be diagnosed with ADHD.

Children who have symptoms of inattention may be easily distracted, may miss key details, may exhibit forgetfulness, and may frequently switch from one activity to another. Such children may also have difficulty focusing on one thing, may become bored with a task prematurely, may have difficulty organizing and completing a task or learning something new, and may be inconsistent with turning in school assignments. Children with symptoms of inattention may not seem to listen when spoken to, may seem to daydream, may exhibit difficulty processing information as accurately as do others, and may have difficulty following instructions.

Children who exhibit symptoms of hyperactivity may fidget and squirm in their seats, may talk continuously, may move about a space quickly, touching or playing with anything in sight, and may have difficulty doing quiet tasks and activities.

Children who exhibit symptoms of impulsivity may be particularly impatient, may blurt out inappropriate comments, and may show their emotions without a normal amount of restraint. These children may also have difficulty waiting their turn and interrupt the conversations and activities of others at a greater than normal level.[11]

Attention deficit hyperactivity disorder can often be mistaken for other problems. Parents and teachers may miss the fact that children have ADHD because they may be quiet. Children with an inattentive form of ADHD may sometimes sit quietly and appear to be working but may not be paying attention to what they are doing.

Attention deficit hyperactivity disorder is one of the most common childhood disorders, and it frequently continues through adolescence into adulthood. It affects about 4.4 percent of American adults age eighteen and older and affects about 9.0 percent of American children aged thirteen to eighteen years.[12] Boys are at four times the risk of ADHD than are girls. Recent studies have shown that the number of children being diagnosed with ADHD is increasing, but the reasons why are not clear.[13]

DIAGNOSING ADHD

Distraction, impulsivity, and extreme levels of energy are natural states that almost all children experience early in their development. From a diagnostic standpoint, sometimes these very normal manifestations of youthful energy can be mistaken for ADHD. Parents and teachers may first notice that their child loses interest in things earlier than other children do or may seem consistently out of control between the ages of three and six. Teachers may consider that students are exhibiting symptoms of ADHD when they have trouble following rules or frequently "space out." Currently, there is no single-test diagnosis for this condition. In order to diagnose a child with ADHD, a pediatrician or mental health specialist will gather information about the child's behavior and environment and will check school and medical records for signs that may be indicators of ADHD. In addition to gathering this information, a physician or specialist will attempt to determine whether the behaviors are excessive and present in the long term, affecting all aspects of the child's life.[14]

Children with ADHD may also have other conditions such as learning disabilities, oppositional defiant disorder, conduct disorder, anxiety and depression, bipolar disorder, or Tourette's syndrome. Learning disabilities take many forms but typically manifest as difficulty understanding sounds or words or as a general struggle with reading, spelling, writing, and math. Children with oppositional defiant disorder are particularly stubborn and may argue with adults while refusing to obey rules. Conduct disorder is a condition in which a child's behaviors may include lying, stealing, fighting, and bullying. Anxiety and depression are occasionally exhibited by children and can be improved through the treatment of ADHD. Some children with ADHD may also have bipolar disorder, in which mood swings range from mania (an extremely elevated mood) to depression in unusually short periods of time.[15] Tourette's syndrome is a brain disorder that is extremely rare among children. Many children with Tourette's syndrome also have ADHD. The symptoms of Tourette's often include nervous ticks and excessively repetitive mannerisms such as eye blinking, facial twitches, and grimacing. Children with Tourette's may clear their throats, snort or sniff frequently, or yell out words inappropriately. Tourette's syndrome can be controlled with medication.[16]

Adults who suspect they have ADHD should be evaluated by a mental health professional who will consider a wide range of symptoms. In order for an adult to be diagnosed with the condition, he or she must exhibit ADHD symptoms that began in childhood and have continued through adulthood.[17]

TREATING ADHD

The treatments currently available for ADHD tend to focus on reducing symptoms and improving functioning. These types of treatments include medication, psychotherapy, behavioral training, or a combination of these treatments. Although many of the symptoms of attention deficit hyperactivity disorder can be improved, there is no cure.

The most common type of medication therapy for children is a so-called stimulant, which typically has a calming effect on young people with ADHD. For many children the stimulant medications reduce hyperactivity and impulsivity and improve a their ability to focus on their work and learning. Stimulant medications may have side effects in children that should be considered carefully. Current medications prescribed for students with ADHD do not cure the disorder but, rather, control symptoms.[18]

A few different types of psychotherapy are used for treating ADHD. Behavioral therapy attempts to help a child change his or her behavior. Behavioral therapy may involve practical assistance such as helping a child organize tasks, complete schoolwork, or work through difficult emotions. The positive or negative feedback given by parents or teachers can be considered a form a behavioral therapy that can include clear rules, expectations, chore lists, and structured routines.[19]

Children with ADHD need special guidance and understanding from their parents and teachers in order to have a successful educational life. Parenting skills training is a useful tool that helps parents use a specific system of rewards and consequences to assist in changing a child's behavior. In this system of behavior modification, parents are taught to give quick, positive feedback for behavior they wish to encourage and to ignore or redirect behavior they wish to discourage. "Time-outs" are typically used when a child's behavior gets out of control. Parenting skills training encourages parents to share a pleasant and relaxing activity with the child and to encourage what the child does well in this activity, rewarding him or her with praise. In addition, therapists can assist family members to find better ways to encourage behavioral changes and can provide

family members. Group therapy for multiple
'en with ADHD is also frequently used.[20]
t hyperactivity disorder in adults is treated much
in that typically a combination of therapies in-
1 and psychotherapy is employed. Although
antidepressants are not formally FDA-approved for the treatment
of ADHD in adults, they are sometimes used.

Children with ADHD often succeed when given a predictable routine. Their day should be strictly scheduled from the moment they wake up to the moment they go to bed, including time for homework, extracurricular activities, playing outdoors, and other activities that the child may enjoy. Keeping a written version of this schedule on a public and visible space in the home can help keep such a routine on track. Changes to their schedule should be written down as far in advance as possible. The organization of everyday items can also assist students with ADHD. Items such as clothing, backpacks, toys, and music books should have a regular place and be put away routinely. School notebooks and homework should be used in an organized way, and children should be encouraged to write down assignments daily. Perhaps most important, children with ADHD should be communicated with clearly and consistently and be given rules that they can understand and follow. When they follow these rules, they should be praised and given small rewards.[21]

TEACHING STUDENTS WITH ADHD

Organizing instruction, planning the lesson, and rewarding focused work are important in teaching any student. The importance of this type of organization for piano lessons with students with ADHD, however, cannot be overstated.

Teaching techniques that tend to help students with ADHD focus and maintain their concentration at the beginning of a lesson may include signaling the start the lesson with an aural cue. In the context of a piano lesson, a "theme song" played by the teacher may prove effective. Listing the activities to be covered during the hour on an easily visible chalk or pen board may help students maintain their focus and prepare for a sequential style of learning. At the beginning of a lesson, tell students clearly and quickly what they're going to learn and what your expectations of them are. Perhaps most important, establish eye contact with students who have ADHD in order to create a sense of focus, trust, and instructional investment from the first minute.

During a lesson, keep instructions simple. Be sure that you are using the fewest words possible to get an instructional point across. Continually vary the tempo of the lesson, including many different kinds of activities. Students with ADHD typically thrive with rapid, intensely paced games that involve competition. A subtle cue can be established in order to remind the student to stay on task. In the context of a piano lesson, this cue may be touching the student lightly on the shoulder, placing a special sticker on his or her book, or playing a tune lightly in the upper registers of the keyboard. Consider allowing a student with ADHD the option of taking breaks during a piano lesson. At the end of a lesson, summarize key points and use the Socratic method to gauge how much of the lesson the student has internalized. Consider having the student write the assignment in his or her notebook, helping the student reiterate the instruction that has occurred.

The importance of clarity in the communication of expectations for effective work with students with ADHD cannot be overstated. I have found that reserving a longer-than-average period of time at the end of the lesson for reviewing assignments is effective, as well as having students write down the steps they should take to practice in the coming week. It is most effective to give piano students with ADHD instructions one at a time, taking the time to repeat these instructions when they may be having trouble processing such information. Because symptoms of inattention and hyperactivity tend to increase over time, it may be useful to work on the most difficult material early in a lesson. Teachers should also consider creating outlines in advance of a lesson, in order to organize the information as it is delivered. A sample outline appears below.

1. Welcome!
    a. How are you?
    b. What was the highlight of your week?
    c. What did you enjoy practicing this week?
2. Sight-Reading
    a. Right hand alone
    b. Left hand alone
    c. Hands together
3. Scales and Arpeggios
    a. Let's hear your scale homework from last week.
    b. Let's hear your arpeggio homework from last week.
    c. Let's learn this week's scale.
    d. Let's learn this week's arpeggio.
4. Pieces
    a. Bach
    b. Copland
5. Review
    a. Please tell me what we worked on today.
    b. Please write your assignments for this week's practicing in your notebook.

Attention deficit hyperactivity disorder can be a challenging diagnosis for students, parents, and teachers alike. With the right toolkit and approach, this diagnosis does not need to be a liability but, rather, can be channeled effectively and positively.

NOTES

1. National Institute of Mental Health, "Attention Deficit Hyperactivity Disorder." Accessed December 20, 2017. https://www.nimh.nih.gov/health/topics/attention-deficit-hyperactivity-disorder-adhd/index.shtml.
2. Centers for Disease Control and Prevention, "Attention-Deficit/Hyperactivity Disorder (ADHD)," August 31, 2017. Accessed December 20, 2017. https://www.cdc.gov/ncbddd/adhd/diagnosis.html.
3. David A. Hay, Kellie S. Bennett, Florence Levy, Joseph Sergeant, and James Swanson, "A Twin Study of Attention-Deficit/Hyperactivity Disorder Dimensions Rated by the Strengths and Weaknesses of ADHD-Symptoms and Normal-Behavior (SWAN) scale," *Biological Psychiatry* 61, no. 5 (2007): 700–705.
4. Ricardo Saute, Kevin Dabbs, Jana E. Jones, Daren C. Jackson, Michael Seidenberg, and Bruce P. Hermann, "Brain Morphology in Children with Epilepsy and ADHD," *PloS One* 9, no. 4 (2014): e95269.
5. Patrick de Zeeuw, F. Zwart, R. Schrama, H. van Engeland, and S. Durston, "Prenatal Exposure to Cigarette Smoke or Alcohol and Cerebellum Volume in Attention-Deficit/Hyperactivity Disorder and Typical Development," *Translational Psychiatry* 2, no. 3 (2012): e84.
6. Lisa M. Chiodo, Sandra W. Jacobson, and Joseph L. Jacobson, "Neurodevelopmental Effects of Postnatal Lead Exposure at Very Low Levels," *Neurotoxicology and Teratology* 26, no. 3 (2004): 359–371.
7. Joan P. Gerring, Beth Slomine, Roma A. Vasa, Marco Grados, Anita Chen, William Rising, James R. Christensen, Martha B. Denckla, and Monique Ernst, "Clinical Predictors of Posttraumatic Stress Disorder after Closed Head Injury in Children," *Journal of the American Academy of Child and Adolescent Psychiatry* 41, no. 2 (2002): 157–165.
8. Mark L. Wolraich, Scott D. Lindgren, Phyllis J. Stumbo, Lewis D. Stegink, Mark I. Appelbaum, and Mary C. Kiritsy, "Effects of Diets High in Sucrose or Aspartame on the Behavior and Cognitive Performance of Children," *New England Journal of Medicine* 330, no. 5 (1994): 301–307.
9. Mark L. Wolraich, David B. Wilson, and J. Wade White, "The Effect of Sugar on Behavior or Cognition in Children: A Meta-Analysis," *Journal of the American Medical Association* 274, no. 20 (1995): 1617–1621.

10. Donna McCann, Angelina Barrett, Alison Cooper, Debbie Crumpler, Lindy Dalen, Kate Grimshaw, Elizabeth Kitchin, et al., "Food Additives and Hyperactive Behaviour in 3-Year-Old and 8/9-Year-Old Children in the Community: A Randomised, Double-Blinded, Placebo-Controlled Trial," *Lancet* 370, no. 9598 (2007): 1560–1567.
11. Manfred Döpfner, Christopher Hautmann, Anja Görtz-Dorten, Fionna Klasen, Ulrike Ravens-Sieberer, and BELLA Study Group, "Long-Term Course of ADHD Symptoms from Childhood to Early Adulthood in a Community Sample," *European Child and Adolescent Psychiatry* 24, no. 6 (2015): 665–673.
12. Ronald C. Kessler, Lenard Adler, Russell Barkley, Joseph Biederman, C. Keith Conners, Olga Demler, Stephen V. Faraone et al. "The Prevalence and Correlates of Adult Adhd in the United States: Results From the National Comorbidity Survey Replication," *The American Journal of Psychiatry* 163, no. 4 (2006): 716–723.
13. Daniel J. Safer, "Is ADHD Really Increasing in Youth?" *Journal of Attention Disorders* 22, no. 2 (2018): 107–115.
14. George J. DuPaul and Gary Stoner, *ADHD in the Schools: Assessment and Intervention Strategies* (New York: Guilford, 2014).
15. Joseph Biederman, Jeffrey Newcorn, and Susan Sprich, "Comorbidity of Attention Deficit Hyperactivity Disorder," *American Journal of Psychiatry* 148, no. 5 (1991): 565.
16. Mu-hong Chen, Ying-sheue Chen, Ju-wei Hsu, Kai-lin Huang, Cheng-ta Li, Wei-chen Lin, Wen-han Chang, et al., "Comorbidity of ADHD and Subsequent Bipolar Disorder among Adolescents and Young Adults with Major Depression: A Nationwide Longitudinal Study," *Bipolar Disorders* 17, no. 3 (2015): 315–322.
17. Breno Matte, Luis Augusto Rohde, J. Blake Turner, Prudence W. Fisher, Sa Shen, Claiton HD Bau, Joel T. Nigg, and Eugenio H. Grevet, "Reliability and Validity of Proposed DSM-5 ADHD Symptoms in a Clinical Sample of Adults," *Journal of Neuropsychiatry and Clinical Neurosciences* 27, no. 3 (2015): 228–236.
18. Rania S. Kattura and M. Lynn Crismon, "Clinically Significant Interactions with Stimulants and Other Non-Stimulants for ADHD." In *Applied Clinical Pharmacokinetics and Pharmacodynamics of Psychopharmacological Agents*, 535–549 (New York: Springer International, 2016).
19. J. Russell Ramsay and Anthony L. Rostain, *Cognitive-Behavioral Therapy for Adult ADHD: An Integrative Psychosocial and Medical Approach* (New York: Routledge, 2014).
20. Lauren M. Haack, Miguel Villodas, Keith McBurnett, Stephen Hinshaw, and Linda J. Pfiffner, "Parenting as a Mechanism of Change in Psychosocial

Treatment for Youth with ADHD, Predominantly Inattentive Presentation," *Journal of Abnormal Child Psychology* 45, no. 5 (2017): 841–855.
21. Sandra Schmiedeler, Frank Niklas, and Wolfgang Schneider, "Symptoms of Attention-Deficit Hyperactivity Disorder (ADHD) and Home Learning Environment (HLE): Findings from a Longitudinal Study," *European Journal of Psychology of Education* 29, no. 3 (2014): 467–482.

Chapter 8

Teaching Undergraduate Pianists

Young people who have the great fortune of receiving an undergraduate education are in perhaps the most formative period of their lives. Typically between eighteen and twenty-two years old, undergraduates are just on their way out of the tumultuous teenage years, the age when children ride the roller coaster of emotions from childhood to adulthood, navigating the establishment of their place and identity in the larger world, a host of types of relationships with peers, increased independence from parents, and expanded responsibilities. Undergraduates are liberated from this chaotic time period, often dramatically, released into a brand-new world where most of the responsibilities of life and decision making rest on them. There are no school bells in college and no parents to wake them and make their breakfast. In class, there often are many fewer assignments, and exams are much more heavily weighted. Classes can be shockingly large, and in these large classes, professors may not know students' names, let alone interact with them personally. Social possibilities are suddenly more liberal. For students who choose to participate, party culture and alcohol are easily accessible. Nationally, about 80 percent of college students use alcohol.[1] Although this figure is large, the number of students who drink moderately and responsibly is actually quite reassuring. Seventy percent of college students report drinking four or fewer drinks, a number typically considered safe, on any one occasion. Given these statistics, undergraduate educators would be advised to widen their view of the stressors and motivating factors in student life beyond the traditional focus of binge drinking.

Undergraduate students also face immense time pressure. At a typical institution they may be in lectures for up to six hours per day. This amount of class time must be reconciled with extracurricular or club activities, part-time employment, social life, exercise and well-being activities, spiritual life, and, in the case of the applied music student, practicing, ensemble rehearsals, and concert attendance. The undergraduate's schedule thus becomes, at best, a dizzying exercise in organization and, at worst, a roadmap to burnout, stress, and anxiety. Furthermore, the undergraduate years are often seen as the final chance to make a decision about one's vocation. Although this viewpoint is clearly not based on the reality of the average adult's working life, it is a pressure that undergraduate students believe is real.

The applied music teacher would be well advised to understand these types of pressures in their students' lives, crafting curricula and mentoring strategies that capture the excitement and sense of possibility experienced during this period while also steering clear of the dangers that students face in such a daunting period. Furthermore, the individualized nature of applied instruction provides a unique opportunity to connect with students in impactful ways that are not usually possible in large lectures. In this chapter I present teaching strategies for the piano professor that reflect best practices in undergraduate education across a number of fields.

THE ART OF TEACHING UNDERGRADUATES

Effective teaching of undergraduates is both an art and a science. Reducing effective instruction down to a qualitative list of best practices would ignore the dynamism and, indeed, performance that are involved in passionate student-centered instruction. Furthermore, even the most highly acclaimed new teachers are too often poorly trained in the art and science of teaching. Unfortunately, it is assumed that a newly hired assistant professor of piano will be an effective teacher because he or she is an outstanding pianist and used to be a student. Becoming an excellent teacher of undergraduates is a lifelong process and a major challenge. It is essential for teachers of undergraduates to assume a humble attitude about what they do and do not know and to seek out mentor teachers who are more experienced and established. The learning curve is steep for any newly hired teacher of undergraduates with regard to a host of curricular issues, including standards and expectations for juries and recitals, departmental culture with regard to practicing, rubrics and other methods for measuring student success in and after school, and the motivation of students in and from diverse demographic settings. An openness to constructive criticism of one's teaching, an awareness of the needs of students, and a willingness to constantly expand one's instructional toolbox are all needed in order to approach instruction with the aim of constant improvement.

The teacher of undergraduates would benefit from understanding a student's previous training as completely as possible. Gathering information about concrete pianistic issues such as technical training including scales and arpeggios studied, exercises and études learned, and repertoire undertaken is a good way to develop an inventory of a student's skills. A simple list does not paint a complete picture of the person's curricular needs, but it does begin to illustrate the seriousness of a student's previous studies, the discipline he or she may or may not have had instilled from an early age, and the appropriate grading of repertoire over a number of years.

WRITING EXERCISE: You will find a sample piano inventory worksheet below. What other questions would you ask on such a form?

Piano Inventory Worksheet

- At what age did you begin studying piano?
- How many hours per day do you practice on average?
- Have you learned all major and minor scales and arpeggios in parallel motion?
- Have you learned all major and minor scales and arpeggios in contrary motion?
- What collections of technical exercises have you studied?
- What études have you studied?
- How often do you practice technical elements like exercises, scales, arpeggios, and études?
- Please list all of the works at the advanced level that you have learned.
- What pieces at the advanced level are you interested in studying?
- How do you feel about your sight-reading skills? (A diagnostic examination of sight-reading may also be administered.)
- Do you feel comfortable improvising in a number of different styles? (A diagnostic examination of improvisation may also be administered.)
- Do you know how to realize a lead sheet?
- Do you know how to realize figured bass?

- Besides classical music, what other styles of music do you perform on the piano?
- Besides classical music, what other styles of music do you regularly listen to?
- Do you compose music, or are you interested in learning to compose?
- What experiences do you have playing chamber music? What chamber music repertoire have you played?
- Have you sung in a choir?
- Have you played in a large instrumental ensemble like an orchestra or a band?
- Do you play any other instruments besides the piano?

The first lesson with an undergraduate student offers an opportunity not only to learn about his or her pianistic strengths and weaknesses but also to begin to learn about the student's learning goals, wider educational life, and current practice regimen. I have found it quite effective to turn first lessons with students into discussions over delicious beverages in a nearby coffee house. In these meetings, I try to demonstrate to students that I am an active and eager listener and try to ask questions more than I give answers. When I do comment, I attempt to monitor the amount of time that I spend speaking, talking in short segments, and reflecting my answers on students with further questions. If a student were to ask me: "When did you realize you wanted to be a piano professor?," instead of speaking extensively about the long history of impactful and caring mentors in my education whom I sought to emulate, I would explain that I feel that teaching is a natural outgrowth of performing and is an essential part of the generational growth and maintenance of our field. I may follow such a comment with a question like "Are you interested in teaching?" In my experience, undergraduate students appreciate the opportunity to speak about their career goals. Though these goals may be a little immature and not entirely based on the reality of their field, evincing an attitude that dreams are respected and cultivated shows them that your work with them is centered on their success and growth, and not on your own glory or ego.

A weekly check-in may be an effective way to stay connected with your students' general well-being and educational progress. I typically start all lessons with undergraduates with the question "What's new?" I find that a few minutes of genuine discussion and listening has a number of benefits. From an instructional standpoint, obtaining context from a student about the successes and failures of his or her week can help you design the next hour. If a student has had a particularly stressful week and practicing has been less than optimal, it may be necessary to strike a particularly sensitive tone, while harnessing that hour for guided practice. Never underestimate the empowering feeling of a piano lesson in which a student feels measurably better at the end of sixty minutes!

With international undergraduates, I find that this sort of pre-lesson conversation provides a venue for students to practice verbal communication on a personal and a professional level. Though almost all institutions require that international students demonstrate a certain level of language proficiency in order to enroll, often those with a sufficient level of English do not have the opportunity to engage in professional conversation. Providing this opportunity will not only sharpen the communication skills that students will need going forward in their education and professional life but can help their sense of confidence and empowerment. A colleague of mine who mainly teaches foreign students has a small pen board attached to her studio wall near the door. If a student does not understand a word during a lesson or in a studio class, my colleague will write this word or short phrase on the pen board. All members of the studio are required to define that word during the coming week. The piano studio becomes a laboratory for English vocabulary, and such skills are useful for presentations in classes, lectures before recitals, and job interviews years down the line. Finally these types of check-in conversations at the start of lessons demonstrate to students that your care for them is real and that your instruction is focused upon their needs and aspirations at all times.

STRATEGIES FOR UNDERGRADUATE LECTURES

Although many professors of piano do the majority of their teaching in the studio in a one-on-one setting, a more traditional mode of lecturing may also be a part of one's undergraduate teaching assignment, whether in studio class, performance hour, or courses in piano literature, piano pedagogy, music theory, or music appreciation. Teachers can use strategies in these settings (and to a certain extent in private lessons) to actively engage students while expanding their ability to think critically and develop problem-solving skills. Some examples of such strategies follow.

Alternate short periods of lecturing with questioning. When delivering information in the form of a traditional lecture, speak in short five-to-seven minute segments followed by questions. Ask your students to write their answers in their notes. For example, when explaining the historical evolution of keyboard instruments and how this evolution may apply to a student's performance of an early Beethoven sonata, you may want to punctuate this discussion with a question like "How do you believe the tonal decay of the early pianoforte relates to how we should perform the opening chords of the sonata op. 13?"

Pose questions with an exemplifier. When explaining a concept, ask a student for his or her opinion regarding that concept. For example, when explaining pedaling nuances in a Chopin nocturne, ask, "Do you feel that a fully depressed pedal in the first measure of the piece is appropriate?"

Use guided practice. Ask students to "practice" a piece they are working on as you quietly listen and observe. Take notes on their practicing methodology. After fifteen or twenty minutes, share your thoughts with them about their practicing approach. Ask them to reflect on how their practicing may become more effective. In the final fifteen minutes of the lesson, ask them to practice the same passages again, employing techniques discussed in the preceding time.

Give an end-of-lesson-quiz. In the concluding minutes of a lecture or lesson, briefly quiz your student on the materials that you covered. Studies show that this sort of intermediate quizzing helps students retain both conceptual and factual materials.

Tell stories. Metaphors and stories, and the utilization of these tools to unlock the creative potential of a young pianist, are priceless teaching tools. Because of the canonical nature of our repertoire, even the best teachers can get bogged down in teaching interpretation in mostly practical terms. Although adhering to compositional detail and appropriate style and teaching practical pianistic essentials are important, the development of an undergraduate's imagination and ability to tell stories is, in my opinion, required. All music involves the communication of stories. The pianists who tell the most compelling stories are the pianists we love. In simplest terms, the major difference between music and any other academic pursuit is the communicative aspect, which is not present in, say, mathematics, despite its beauty. Reflecting with undergraduate students about the story, feeling, and narrative present in music can help them connect deeply and personally to their art. Ideally, we are not hoping to create "parrots" that simply mimic our interpretations but conduits of a very personal imaginative impulse. I find that a few very simple exercises can help in this regard. When a student is clearly not connecting emotionally to a portion of a work, I ask, "If this were the music for a movie soundtrack, what would be happening in this scene?" Inevitably, for a student who is reluctant to come forward with an answer, I would ask more specific guided questions. "Is the scene in this movie happening inside, or outside?" "Is this outside place cold or warm?" "At what time of year is this scene happening?" "Who is there?" "Is this scene sunny or cloudy?" "Is this the desert or the seaside?" The possibilities for guided questions in a situation like this are endless. You would do well to build your supply of illustrations and guided questions in order to engage a student's creative center.

IMAGINATION EXERCISE: Have your student choose a piece they are currently working on. Have them write a short piece of fiction that might describe this piece. Encourage them to be as detailed as possible when describing the emotions and sensory imagery of this piece. Have them describe specifically how their narrative connects with specific elements of and moments in the piece.

Ask questions that stimulate thinking. Asking the right kinds of questions can open the door to critical thinking for an undergraduate. Carefully crafted questions focus a student's attention on applying his or her current knowledge to specific content or to a new problem. Effective questions create avenues of discovery, elicit follow-up questions and lines of inquiry, and lead to deeper and more impactful understanding of a given concept. Sometimes, this type of teaching through questioning is referred to as the Socratic method. Questions created in this way do not rely on the recall of facts and information but, rather, teach a student how to think critically. The following are examples of types of questions that could create learning and discovery using the Socratic method:

> Generalization: "How do we apply phrasing and gesture principles from Mozart in Chopin?"
>
> Prediction: "In his Opus 13 sonata, Beethoven has created a sense of harmonic anticipation as we approach the coda of the third movement. What do you predict will happen next? Is your prediction correct? How does he defy conventional prediction in this moment? How does Beethoven's defiance of convention affect how you will interpret the end of this piece? How does Beethoven's defiance affect the way the audience experiences this ending?"
>
> Possibilities: "How many different ways can you shape this phrase?" "How many different articulations can you employ in this melody?" "What if you try to play this section significantly faster than the previous section?" "What if you try to play this section significantly slower than the previous section?" "How many different types of pedaling are possible in this phrase?" "What happens to the sound if you use a half una corda pedaling in this section?" "Can you surprise me as a listener with how long you hold this fermata?" "Can you surprise me as a listener with how briefly you hold this fermata?" "Is it possible for you to employ silence and rests in this section in such a way that their impact is as strong as your accents?"
>
> Analogy: "What do the descending figures in this right-hand passage sound like to you?" "What do you think the composer was experiencing in her life when she wrote this?" "If this passage were a flower, what color would it be?" "Can you play this passage like the smell of freshly cut grass in June?"

Reflection: "As you have prepared and memorized this movement, what have you found particularly interesting? How did Beethoven surprise you with his unconventional use of sonata-allegro form?"

Detailed description: "Tell me, in detail, about the harmonic progression of this movement." "How does Schumann unfold the drama in this work?" "Tell me about the texture of the left hand. How does it twist and turn? Is the texture dense or transparent?"

HELPING UNDERGRADUATES DEVELOP CRITICAL THINKING SKILLS

Successfully engaging undergraduate learners is critical to creating buy-in and establishing problem-solving skills, independent critical thinking, and a love of learning. Teachers of undergraduates can promote and encourage these traits in their students with well-timed and carefully crafted positive feedback. Although on the surface positive feedback sounds like something that should be shared liberally with students, especially students early in their careers in higher education, it can be a detriment to good learning and study habits when delivered with hollowness or insincerity. Some good rules of thumb for positive reinforcement are outlined below.

Avoid using empty praise. Praise, by definition, is an absolute judgment. The use of praise in an educational setting such as a piano lesson may cause the student to seek approval from the teacher rather than seeking to become an independent learner. Rather than using such phrases as "Nice playing," "Good work," or "I like how solid this is sounding," use specific descriptions of a student's performance that address aspects of the student's music making that have needed support: "You have improved the pedaling as we discussed in last week's lesson. Thank you." "It is clear to me that you have practiced the left hand alone as I suggested to you and your classmates in studio class." "The clarity of your phrasing is greatly improved. Because of this, the story you are trying to weave together here is much more coherent and compelling."

When attempting to give positive reinforcement, never underestimate the power of nonverbal cues. Most people are quite attuned to nonverbal cues and tend to glean just as much information from facial expressions and body language as they do from speech. When you are expressing joy about a student's progress, be sure that you are smiling enthusiastically and honestly. When coupled with a simple thumbs up or a bit of applause, a positive assessment can be amplified significantly.

Describing your personal feelings in response to a student's performance, or a particularly passionate discussion in class, can be effective in engaging and positively reinforcing a student's work. For example, you could say, "It is such a joy for me to listen to you play this music!" or "Today, I am truly amazed by your progress." The judicious use of personal emotion can help students feel pride in their work, done not just for a teacher's approval but for the achievement of much broader learning goals and self-efficacy.

In fact, self-efficacy, self-satisfaction, and feelings of self-worth are critical to an undergraduate student's growth as an increasingly independent learner. There is great power in a teacher's providing praise that is designed to nurture and cultivate these sorts of feelings about the self. A teacher can positively reinforce the concept of growth: "Your recital tonight represents a significant step forward in your development as a pianist. I imagine that must be a wonderful feeling." A teacher can positively reinforce the concept of enjoyment: "I had a lot of fun listening to your dress rehearsal. I can't imagine how excited you are about your senior recital." A teacher can positively reinforce the concept of competence: "After all of that hard work, your scales and arpeggios are now excellent. You must be so satisfied with your hard work."

OPPORTUNITIES FOR ACTIVE LEARNING

Active learning is a cornerstone of successful learners in higher education. Active learning may be particularly important to young pianists who spend a much larger percentage of their time on their own in a practice room than they do with their professor. The following are some strategies for delivering instruction in ways that foster active learning.

The studio class or group lesson is a particularly effective venue for group problem-solving. As an example, if a student were to have a memory problem in a studio class performance, you could engage classmates in developing strategies alongside the performer. First and foremost, a caution: performance is a vulnerable pursuit. It is entirely possible that students in a studio will not have the rapport and friendship needed to engage in this type of activity. If they do, however, ask the group about how to improve memory in performance. You might say, "First of all, I would like to congratulate Natsumi on persisting through her performance. Memorization security in performance is a process, and part of that process is making memory mistakes in front of an audience. Natsumi, you shouldn't be ashamed, but rather, you should be thankful that you more intimately know your level of preparation and what things you need to address before you take this piece on to the stage. Now, what are some specific ways that Natsumi can practice this Beethoven sonata to shore up her memory?" When the group dynamic is positive and supportive, the type of discussion that may follow might prove to be a workshop on memory issues for the studio. Rather than a teacher simply giving out information, students could provide a list of practicing strategies that have worked for them, while attempting to develop new strategies based on the piece being performed. This type of active learning not only draws students into the discussion of problem-solving but also gives students ownership over their contributions, and helps them establish a toolkit for their own teaching in the future.

In an undergraduate course in piano pedagogy, the use of a "concept model" may be particularly effective. The instructor, for example, could distribute a handout that asks a series of leading questions about young students' practicing habits at home. Effective questions may be similar to the following: "Eight-year-old Bryce is rarely prepared for his lessons. It has become clear to you that your student, Bryce, rarely practices at home, despite testimonies to the contrary by his parents. What do you feel your role is as Bryce's teacher in confronting this situation? What are some tactics for helping Bryce establish a more regular and effective practice routine at home that is supported by his parents?" After receiving their handouts, students could break into small groups to create models, lists, or diagrams of systems that would address the scenario and answer the guided questions you have provided. After a period of time in the small groups, students could tell the larger group what they would suggest in this particular situation and how they came to these conclusions. Engaging undergraduates' thought process in such a way can be a powerful means of supporting independent thinking, group work that utilizes compromise, and the working-out of real-world situations that may one day be applied in the teaching studio.

A simulation is a powerful teaching tool to use with the undergraduate pianist, especially one who is not particularly experienced in the art of performing. I find that creating opportunities to simulate the pressures and realities of performing on stage are critical for preparing the performing pianist. On a micro level, the weekly lesson should in some way represent the high level of pressure and even, in tolerable and supportive doses, the nervousness associated with a high-stakes performance. Teachers of undergraduates may seek to support such a model with specific playing assignments: in every lesson build on the scaffolding of a semester-long set of goals, offer opportunities for weekly lessons to be videorecorded or attended by other members of the studio in order to somewhat simulate the presence of an audience, and, though this may seem extreme to some, impose a dress code.

In my studio, students may perform a complete movement in a lesson once with a score. On second hearing, the movement or piece must be performed from memory. On third hearing, they must present this work in studio class, which is held on the same stage where their recitals and recital approvals are held. My aim with such standards is simple: Students are consistently expected to move forward with their preparation of repertoire and études in a way that simulates the pressures of the performing pianist. Music must move from a place of extensive score study, familiarity, and comfort to a place where it is initially written on the hard drive of the mind. Such an accelerated schedule may seem stressful, but when presented in a way that is clearly supported by a caring and student-centered instructor, such a structure can lead to improvements in the efficiency of learning new repertoire, sight-reading skills, and security in memorization. Furthermore, a "real-world" set of standards as described above will prepare undergraduate students for the realities of graduate school and a professional life, in which a large and diverse repertoire must be prepared simultaneously. Opening up at least a portion of the piano lesson to other students identified as supportive colleagues can simulate the pressures of performance while also offering learning experiences for all the students present.

The eminent piano professor and concert artist Leon Fleisher famously teaches all of his students with his entire studio present. In such a situation, students have the opportunity to learn about multiple pieces in the vast piano repertoire without having the pressure of delivering a performance.

Teachers may consider having a dress code in order to more effectively simulate the specific feeling of a performance. My piano professor, Daniel Pollack, would require students to wear portions of their concert outfits that might impact performance in the final lessons that led up to a recital. I will never forget the valuable lesson this taught me about the tightness of a suit jacket or the slickness of a pair of dress shoes. Doing this a number of times took the surprise out of those feelings when it was time to take the stage. I am aware of teachers who forbid students to dress casually for weekly lessons. Although a rule like this may not realistically be implemented in many modern piano studios, its benefits are obvious. Casual dress and attitudes in a piano lesson do not simulate the seriousness, preparation, and execution of the concert stage.

The opportunity to participate in peer teaching can be fruitful for undergraduate students. Peer teaching can take a number of different forms in a piano studio. For example, juniors and seniors in a studio may find the mentoring of younger studio members to be an opportunity to sharpen their teaching skills. An instructor might consider assigning senior members of a studio to a number of mentoring tasks including mini technique lessons (perhaps fifteen-minute lessons each week in which scales, arpeggios, exercises, and études are checked on), shadow teaching (in which senior members of a studio attend lessons of junior members, with the opportunity to teach younger members for a portion of the lesson), substitute teaching while an instructor is away, or studio members giving each other constructive feedback during a studio class or group lesson. In order to be a success, this type of teaching would need to be coached by the instructor in a setting where all students involved understand the learning goals and desired outcomes.

These models of peer teaching have a number of potential benefits for undergraduate students, whether involved as students or teachers. The reality of our profession is that almost all musicians who wish to make a living as an artist must teach. This is not an indication of desperation on the part of aspiring young pianists but, rather, a beautiful reality that keep our profession alive and the next generation of young pianists in good hands! Modeling good teaching is one thing, but providing students the opportunity to get their feet wet with the teaching of advanced students is priceless. The benefits of peer teaching for undergraduates don't stop with those who are teaching. Senior members of a studio who are teaching junior members learn the importance of collegiality, lesson planning, and the careful execution and realization of a teaching plan. We are all lifelong learners and teachers. Traditions of great teachers are handed down from master teachers and performers through experiences like peer teaching.

MODELS OF EVALUATION

Traditionally, the model of evaluation for undergraduate pianists is limited to end-of-semester juried examinations. Undergraduates may also encounter barrier juries after the sophomore or junior year, exit juries or senior recital approvals, or separate technique juries extracted from the performance of repertoire for a grade. The model of an infrequent but heavily weighted examination schedule may have significant drawbacks for undergraduates, who are used to a high school examination timetable that might include much more frequent testing. I find that providing graded examinations almost weekly on very specific material near the beginning of an undergraduate's career provides a better scaffolding of accountability, task division, and pacing of preparation on which students can build personal accountability and independent learning skills. Grading of preparation for a weekly lesson is another useful tool. Furthermore, having the student grade his or her own weekly lesson may provide significant opportunities for meaningful self-reflection and ownership of practicing habits. I have asked particular students to provide a one-page written evaluation and grade following each of their lessons during their undergraduate training. Working with students in such a manner has proved to be an effective way to partner with them in their preparation for accountability.

A useful technique for working with undergraduate students in a positive mentoring relationship is establishing agreed-on goals and objectives, which logically become clearly articulated criteria for grading. Unfortunately, applied piano teachers establish such a systematic approach to developing course outcomes in a syllabus less frequently than do classroom teachers. A useful syllabus will clearly connect learning objectives and goals to grades, explaining, in detail, how each possible grade can be attained. If a piano department has multiple faculty members, it would be wise for all faculty members to establish common views about what specific learning goals for undergraduate pianists should be. Although the learning process itself is clearly where the bulk of knowledge attainment takes place, grading a process rather than outcomes can be tricky. A successfully designed undergraduate syllabus in piano will measure outcomes rather than processes. For example, a process-oriented statement in a piano performance syllabus might read, "Students will study two contrasting works and an étude during the course of the semester," whereas an outcome-oriented statement might read, "Students will give a jury performance of two contrasting works and an étude, which will be evaluated by the entire piano faculty."

Another important aspect of connecting goals and learning outcomes to grades is providing detailed descriptions of assignments and assessments in a clearly delineated syllabus *in writing*. I know many professors of undergraduate piano who do not offer their students a formal syllabus but instead rely on verbally discussed expectations and assessments. The one-on-one relationship in an applied piano setting carries a certain amount of power in its occasional informality, but distributing a written syllabus at the beginning of each semester provides a framework for students to plan and schedule their work. In addition, most institutions require that instructors provide a syllabus for each student.

WRITING EXERCISE: Obtain the syllabi of the piano professors at your school. Design a syllabus for a first-year piano performance major.

MODELING ENTHUSIASM FOR ACADEMIA

Perhaps the most powerful opportunity to positively affect undergraduate students is through the modeling of an enthusiastic academic life. In my experiences as a teacher at four-year universities and community colleges, I have come to understand that not all students are enthusiastic learners. These attitudes about learning may result from circumstance, natural instinct, or previous instructional modeling, but undergraduate instructors should understand that students may not be as enthusiastic as they were at that age. I believe that it is critical for teachers to model excitement, openness, genuine care, and awe for the voyage of discovery that learning is. Although the music professor's life is often a grueling balance of performance, scholarship, service, travel, practicing, and family life, exhibiting negativity about what is truly a fortunate life of learning and teaching can pass on unfortunate attitudes about one's vocation. Effective teachers are passionate, are constantly open to learning new things, are authentic in their interactions, are above the fray of political in-fighting, are open about mistakes they have made, have genuine trust in each of their students, and believe that their students can be the next great minds in their field. Many of the greatest professors I have known have understood that those under their mentorship will someday far surpass all of their own achievements, yet show no element of being threatened by their students' successes.

I was deeply moved by a recent masterclass I witnessed by Leon Fleisher. In working with three students who played very well but clearly at levels lower than those he would accept in his own studio, he showed genuine and palpable respect for each of the students at the conclusion of their performances. He remarked, "I have only deep respect for what you just did. It is amazing that you put yourself on the line in front of probably 1,000 people, as well as me. This shows all of us that you are a serious voice in our field," and also said, "Wow. The level of pianists just continues to climb and climb. I am very excited by this prospect." In his skillful delivery, these lines were not empty praise but truthful and specific tokens of gratitude for the hard work and risk-taking these students had exhibited. Fleisher honored these students in front of curious onlookers, developed an instant trust and rapport with these students for the fifteen minutes in which they would be working with him, and primed an openness and sense of inquiry in the minds of these young people, who might now be more willing to accept constructive criticism and suggestions for artistic change. This was not candy-coated instruction but, rather, mutual inquiry brought about, in part, by skillful modeling of an academic and artistic life that was candid and sincere.

MAINTAINING A SAFE AND PROFESSIONAL RELATIONSHIP

The subject of providing an effective and safe climate for learning is critical for undergraduate learning done in such a potentially dangerous venue as the private lesson. In such lessons, often taught in offices behind closed doors, a power dynamic between an instructor and a student is clearly present. Students must never feel as if a professor will take advantage of such a setting in any way, including performing inappropriate or illegal activities or activities that demean a student and make that student feel powerless. It is critical that professors respect the personal physical space of all learners at all times. Many institutions have rules and regulations about physical contact between professors and students, even when such physical contact is part of instruction, as may be the case with the learning of an instrument. A professor must be aware of any such rules at his or her institution and not only abide by them but take to heart the reasons for their existence. In the absence of such rules, a professor needs to be guided by the student in terms of consent for any physical touch at all. There are times when I find it useful to guide a student's wrist at the keyboard, place his or her hand on the piano correctly, or somehow help with physical orientation toward the instrument. I always abide by a system of asking the student first, "Are you comfortable with me touching your hand? I will understand if you are not, and I will find another way to explain this." The reasons for someone not being comfortable with physical contact are myriad, but respecting a student's opinion about such a matter is essential.

Furthermore, an undergraduate teacher of piano would be well advised to meet students' needs for both physical comfort and accessibility in the teaching studio. A pleasant space that features adequate lighting, appropriate sound isolation, and a generally relaxing atmosphere will help a student feel supported and open to instruction. When a comfortable space is paired with an instructor who clearly establishes his or her role as a facilitator of learning, the pursuit of knowledge can unfold in a mutually beneficial way. Students should be clearly informed that their teacher is not the ultimate authority and fount of all related knowledge. Such a situation may inflate the ego of the instructor, making him or her feel temporarily omniscient, but such a power dynamic is disingenuous, dangerous, unsustainable, and, ultimately, self-serving. Student-centered instruction centers on an instructor's facilitating a student's voyage toward a responsibility for his or her own learning. In my pedagogy classes, I like to describe this as "teaching yourself out of a job." Instructors support students, come along with them in their quest for answers, point them gently in the right direction, and remove the "training wheels" so that students are not only inspired to search for answers themselves but are excited to inspire the next generation of searchers. In the context of an undergraduate piano curriculum, learning facilitation may include allowing students to create their own imaginative interpretations of pieces, encouraging students to develop entrepreneurial initiatives including service and performance opportunities in the community, or the creation of student-run clubs such as a collegiate chapter of the Music Teachers National Association. Information about starting a collegiate chapter can be found at http://www.mtna.org/collegiate-chapters/.

LEARNER RESPONSIBILITY

Learner responsibility is perhaps the most important guiding principle of quality undergraduate instruction. Four years is a very short amount of time in which to transition from the strictly monitored, step-by-step type of learning that takes place in many high schools to the significant liberty in research and assignments found in graduate school or the workplace. Designing instruction in these four years with this ultimate goal in mind can help frame learning and exploration in ways that guide a student toward independence. Some specific suggestions for undergraduate piano instruction are given below.

First, involve students in lesson and repertoire planning. Like most applied piano instructors, I gather repertoire lists from students at the beginning of their study with me and add to this list as the years go by. My hope in such a system is to broadly expose them to the wide and diverse piano repertoire available to us from all periods and cultures. In addition, I ask students what pieces they are hoping to study in their time in my studio. If the pieces they mention both meet the repertoire needs I see in their list of pieces studied and are developmentally appropriate (slightly more challenging than the pieces they are currently working on), I will encourage them to play these exact works. If the works do not meet most of these qualifications, I might suggest a work that involves similar types of playing or is by the same or a similar composer. For example, if a typical-level college freshman piano performance major states that she wants to learn the Liszt sonata, I might suggest that she study the Liszt Concert Etudes in her first year. This particular suggestion honors and reflects the student's predilection for the High Romantic style of music while choosing a work by the requested composer. Moreover, the Concert Etudes, which might be considered a "stepping stone" to much more difficult works by Liszt, do not come across as remedial in any sense. The music is challenging to the performer, engaging for the listener, and important in the canon of nineteenth-century piano works. Partnering with a student in this sort of carefully considered choice may make the student feel committed and invested in her work.

Second, engage students in establishing learning goals based on their needs. While an experienced teacher may be able to quickly identify areas in which student need improvement, if done together with students, such a diagnosis can support a self-responsibility model of undergraduate learning. I find that periodic discussion-lessons in which students are encouraged to assess themselves as pianists can be quite powerful. Following a recital or jury, I will ask students to reflect on their performance, first outlining strengths in that performance and then outlining potentials areas for growth. A key element to the former is a discussion of success attribution, that is, asking students why the areas of success they identified occurred. When students correctly and easily identify success with hard work, it is encouraged in future educational endeavors. Another useful exercise is to have students listen to or watch a recording of their performance in a lesson, reflecting on that performance in the objective manner of someone speaking in the third person. Furthermore, I will occasionally record students performance and ask them to review their performance and reflect on it in the form of a short written response in prose form, focusing on concepts such as clarity of intention, interpretive voice, and delivery of imaginative concept.

Third, partner with students to establish their learning objectives. I find that contracts with students, based on learning goals related to portions of the course requirements as outlined in a syllabus, may help learners see a path from an area needing improvement to their specific learning goal, find effective strategies for attaining goals, and establish how a performance at the end of the semester jury will be evaluated.

Finally, consider involving your students in the evaluation of their learning. Although it may seem like a radical and possibly ill-advised concept to ask students to grade themselves, such an exercise can prove valuable guided so that it is an honest and deep-thinking evaluation of one's effort and advancement and not just an opportunity to pad one's grade point average. After a performance jury, I typically meet with all of my students one-on-one for about thirty minutes. I present them with the comments written by other members of the piano faculty and ask them to grade their jury performance based on these reactions *and their own*. After completing this short exercise, I ask them what grade they might deserve for their effort and work during the bulk of the semester. Furthermore, I ask them to justify both grades, describing the reasons why they believe they deserve the grades that they have suggested. Almost always, the grades that undergraduate students provide to me in these situations are exactly what I would assign them independently (and typically for the same reasons that they outline). Student-supplied grades that are either too inflated or too low present a valuable opportunity for a discussion about appropriate self-evaluation in which concepts of self-worth may arise. Partnering with students to determine their grade for the semester can turn evaluation into yet another venue for instruction and the exploration of knowledge and academic responsibility.

NOTE

1. National Institute on Alcohol Abuse and Alcoholism, "College Drinking." Accessed June 14, 2018. https://pubs.niaaa.nih.gov/publications/collegefactsheet/Collegefactsheet.pdf.

Chapter 9

Mentoring Graduate Student Pianists

Graduate study in piano is a wide and diverse field. In many colleges, universities, and conservatories in the United States, multiple graduate degree programs exist that serve a variety of types of students and needs in the fields of piano performance and piano pedagogy. At the master's level, degree programs are widely distributed in solo and collaborative performance, as well as piano pedagogy. At the doctoral level, degree programs exist at even more varied levels and within even more varied traditions within the historical academy, including doctor of musical arts programs in solo piano, doctor of musical arts programs in collaborative piano, doctor of musical arts programs in piano pedagogy and doctor of philosophy programs in education with an emphasis on piano pedagogy. While rigor and degree requirements vary from school to school, a line of distinction is generally drawn between the emphasis on performance of doctor of musical arts programs and the emphasis on research and writing of doctor of philosophy programs. Furthermore, specific schools may have philosophical goals for their training of pianists and piano teachers, be those goals the training of concert artists, chamber musicians, teachers of group piano, teachers of solo piano, teachers of young beginners, or teachers of adult recreational students. It is impossible to speak specifically to the teaching of graduate students in piano when the students in this field are approaching such a broad range of programs. Rather than addressing all of these fields of study individually, in this chapter I speak more generally of the unique mentoring relationship that a teacher of graduate students has with his or her mentees, addressing best practices for mentoring across a variety of fields. Fortunately, in many cases these practices are nearly universal for effective instruction, so studying them and their genesis is not a fruitless endeavor but, rather, has application for a number of types of teaching.

A BRIEF HISTORY OF GRADUATE EDUCATION

The tradition of graduate education can be traced back to medieval European universities. In these settings, "undergraduate" study typically involved six years of schooling, with up to twelve more years for the equivalent of master's and doctor's degrees. In the ancient world, undergraduate education involved the study of the seven liberal arts: rhetoric, logic, grammar, music theory, astronomy, geometry, and arithmetic. (How fascinating that music theory was a core subject of the ancient liberal education. We clearly have something to gain from the study of the ancients!) Once a bachelor's degree was received, a student could choose one of three fields to study at the graduate level: theology, medicine, or law. Master's and doctor's degrees were often equivalent in the ancient world, with distinctions made between particular universities or geographical areas and level of academic achievement. Typically, master's degrees were more frequently awarded in Paris and at universities under the influence of this system, with doctoral degrees more common in

Bologna and universities related to this tradition. At Oxford and Cambridge, the study of law, medicine, or theology usually was indicated with the title of doctor, while the title of master was used for all other fields. In medieval Europe, theology was normally thought of as the most important subject in the academy, driving the concept of the doctorate's being considered the more prominent degree above the masters. For many countries that have generally inherited the British model, the master's degree was the only graduate degree awarded, while in European countries other than the United Kingdom, the master's degree nearly disappeared. In the second half of the nineteenth century, universities in the United States began to emulate the European model by awarding doctorates, this practice eventually spreading to the United Kingdom.[1]

THE ROLE OF MENTOR

Graduate education is now typically driven by trends in the academic marketplace in the United States, which tends to determine current traditions in graduate education and research. In many fields mentoring, in the form of a professor's working with a single graduate student, is employed when it comes to research guidance, teacher training, job search assistance, and more generally the modeling of a successful and vibrant academic life. It is interesting to see the way in which the mentoring of graduate students mimics the applied teaching of piano students at all levels, including a one-on-one weekly meeting, full attention given to a student during an instructional period, the supervision of specific academic projects, and the frequently encountered counseling relationship afforded in such a setting. I have not seen any evidence that applied music instruction influenced the typical graduate student–mentor relationship, but considering the predominance of music theory in the canon of required academic fields in the medieval academy, perhaps such a relationship is possible. Whatever the initial impetus of graduate mentoring, this relationship is worth exploring and that skilled and successful mentors of graduate students will abide by principles that perpetuate the concept of the development of academic independence taught at the undergraduate level, while helping mentees hone the skills of teaching, research, discipline expansion, and job training that often are required when working with graduate students in music.

Whereas driven professors of music will be actively involved in the pursuit of knowledge and the production of artistic products that push the boundaries of their art to previously unknown places, those same individuals will be asked to be effective and selfless mentors to a group of graduate students of varying levels and abilities. Effective mentors of graduate students will be multifaceted and multitalented. These individuals may aim to embody a certain set of attributes, including the following.

- Taking a genuine interest in developing another individual's career
- Having a relationship with an individual that is simultaneously personal and professional
- Being willing to develop an individual's academic and professional goals in ways that are directed by the mentee
- Being willing to adjust mentoring styles and curricular content in ways that reflect the increasingly diverse and multicultural landscape of modern higher education

The concept of a mentor implies that a professor is seeking to play a role that is above and beyond simply that of an advisor or of a piano teacher. Mentoring implies playing an expanded role in the life of a student in order to develop a future colleague. The role of an advisor or of the average graduate-level piano teacher is to successfully guide academic and musical progress, while the role of a mentor reflects a professor's commitment to developing a graduate student's career by the use of personal care, experience, and expertise in the field of piano performance and teaching.

Much as students have different learning styles, the skills and strengths of mentors of graduate students are varied. There is no one single formula for mentoring graduate student pianists successfully. Multiple approaches and combinations of approaches will be applied by a mentor with a keen intellect and open and honest mind about the needs of a student. This chapter does not seek to outline one ultimate approach to mentoring but to outline some suggested approaches that have worked in some way. An innovative professor who seeks to be an effective mentor may combine and distill a number of these approaches in a way that may effectively reach a specific type of graduate student.

THE BENEFITS OF MENTORING GRADUATE STUDENTS

The benefits for the graduate teacher of piano of becoming an effective mentor are clear. Mentoring both benefits students and advances the discipline of piano performance and teaching by modeling quality instruction and commitment to high-level piano pedagogy in the professors of the next generation. Mentoring provides specific benefits to students in the academy, including, perhaps most important, the assurance that someone with greater influence than they possess cares about their positive progress and that this person will give advice in difficult situations. Graduate students may be facing significant anxiety about a host of issues related to their schooling, their future life as a professional in the fickle field of music, and their personal life. Having someone they can rely on for advice and advocacy may help alleviate some of these stressors. Mentors may have access to networks and professional connections that students may not yet have. Assisting graduate students build connections within your professional network may not only help kick-start their career but also may be a way to build confidence and trust in the mentoring relationship by demonstrating a willingness to establish such connections. Graduate study can often be a time when unexpected circumstances related to study bring surprise visits. An effective mentor will not only lay out a schedule of milestone events in the graduate student's life (recitals, comprehensive exams, proposals, presentations, papers, or defenses) but will describe in detail the specific nature of each of these exercises. Examples include giving solid advice about which faculty members would be most helpful on a committee, the timing of recitals tailored to a student's learning speed and style, how to develop a proposal for a conference (as well as which conferences to attend), and how to most effectively study and prepare for a comprehensive examination.

The mentoring relationship has benefits for the mentor as well. One of the beauties of being an educator is how much we learn from our students. In the teaching of graduate students, this stream tends to flow up toward professors more than does working with undergraduates, simply because of the high level of commitment and expertise that is required of graduate students. They can help a professor be aware of new findings in the field. I find that my graduate students are more quickly aware of new technologies and resources in piano pedagogy, as well as exciting new young pianists on the world stage. In many research institutions, the success of a professor's mentees is a highly regarded marker in tenure and promotion decisions as well as merit pay. Their obtaining great jobs reflects very positively on their professor. As graduate students become successful scholars, they build their own networks and connections. Staying in touch with them as they reach this stage in their career may expand your own network exponentially. Graduate students in piano are remarkably well connected in both informal and formal ways via avenues of communication like social media and more traditional methods. As the reputation of a mentor grows, students quickly find out and are drawn to that professor.

In the world of graduate-level piano study, some of the most successful recruiters are not necessarily professors whose research and creative activity are the greatest but, rather, those whose reputations have grown within piano teaching circles as caring, connected, and engaged mentors of graduate students.

Perhaps most important, mentoring is personally enriching. Seeing your students launched into the professional world with enthusiasm is very gratifying. Seeing them change and expand your field is rewarding and enhances its richness. While piano teaching is not the fast-breaking field that some of the more traditional sciences are, the addition of qualified instructors and artists creates a landscape where the art and pursuit of playing the piano is not only done at a higher level but also is more accessible in our society.

THE RESPONSIBILITIES OF THE MENTOR

The mentor's responsibilities are incredibly diverse and go well beyond the concept of simply being an effective teacher and supervisor of scholarship. First and foremost, mentors are models of a successful, meaningful, and ethical life in the discipline. Mentors of graduate students in piano will, themselves, be joyful students of the piano repertoire, will be positive and generous collaborators, and will be dedicated and passionate teachers of the instrument, modeling these traits with dignity and commitment. More specifically, they will assist students with developing their professional profile and should be able to define and explain the professional life of a music professor, which may include varied types of teaching, participation in faculty governance and committee work, obtaining funding for creative projects, managing the affairs of a piano studio, and community service. In addition, mentors should model an active and contributing life in professional organizations such as the Music Teachers National Association, the statewide and local MTNA organizations, and the Frances Clark Center for Keyboard Pedagogy.

Mentors of graduate-level pianists should assist students with developing a daily schedule that represents an effective use of time. One of the great hazards and, at the same time, great blessings of graduate school is the sudden freedom of one's schedule. The number of required courses typically is much lower than for an undergraduate, ensemble responsibilities may be more limited, and other aspects of one's academic schedule may suddenly be much freer than they were at the undergraduate level. It is critical that mentors of graduate student pianists help them with developing schedules for meeting both performance and academic deadlines as well as for teaching responsibilities they might have and for larger projects such as conference proposals, comprehensive examinations, and final papers.

Unfortunately, expectations in academia are often convoluted and even vague. It can be difficult for students to navigate such a landscape. The applied teacher of graduate pianists can clarify these types of situations by making expectations clear in a variety of areas, including the timing and content of recitals, coursework required and encouraged, the timing and content of comprehensive examinations, and expectations regarding accompanying and teaching responsibilities.

An effective mentor of graduate students in piano will, above all, model professional integrity on a very high level. In the world of piano teaching one sometimes encounters large egos and self-serving attitudes. Professors who model a commitment to the music, an avoidance of conflicts of interest, a team player attitude when collaborating with faculty colleagues, and a general sense of ethics and standards tend to succeed in attracting a greater quantity and quality of graduate students. He or she will be a joyous consumer of music, someone who might show exhilaration and sense of awe when it comes to the consumption of the daily bread of piano repertoire and pedagogy.

BEST PRACTICES FOR MENTORS

Clarity of expectations is essential for a mentoring relationship. It should go without saying that the boundary between a personal and a professional relationship should be clearly articulated from the outset. Blending a personal and a professional mentoring relationship, though possible, creates a hosts of difficulties in an academic setting. All the same, mentors should be fully accessible to their students. I tell my students that my office door is always open to them. I am easily reachable and open, and I let students know that their access to me in a professional sense is limitless. I attempt to let students understand that I am extremely busy with a very full teaching schedule, frequent travel, a demanding family life, and more. Yet my policy is to respond within twenty-four hours to all student requests, whether they are professional or personal. When meeting with graduate students, I attempt to be fully present. Whether we are meeting for fifteen minutes or two hours, my full attention is them and their current academic topic. As professors, our days are compartmentalized and even fragmented; effective mentors will consider their time spent with graduate students as sacred, perhaps more so than with students at other levels, because these students are on the verge of being let loose into our field.

Good mentors will have a reliable system for keeping track of their students' achievements. Many universities utilize a merit-pay system in which professors must report their annual activities, a large portion of which consists of the activities and progress of their graduate students. It is important to let them know from the outset that you want them to succeed professionally, and indicating specific ways in which they can do this can set up an atmosphere of achievement and growth. In my mentorship, I let students know at the beginning of their studies at the master's level in piano pedagogy that presenting their teaching and research at state-level, national, and international venues is an essential step in their professional development. They will benefit from the honing of proposal and presentation skills, the expansion of their professional networks, and the sharpening of preparation and presenting skills at conferences. Effective mentors will make a conscious effort to reward and recognize these achievements, and, further, will see that they are reflected in reports within the studio, graduate program, or unit of study as well as in the reports required of faculty members related to promotion and merit achievement.

A mentor will be sensitive and supportive when it comes to both success and discouragement. Emotional distress, anxiety, and depression are all conditions that students may bring with them to graduate school. When students need help, they will not necessarily ask for it. When they are not working up to the standard you expect, there may be underlying causes and not simply a lack of commitment and drive. Openness to exploring issues that may be decreasing productivity is an essential trait in an effective mentor.

ESTABLISHING A MENTORING RELATIONSHIP

For better or for worse, much of our practice and behavior as teachers, performers, scholars, and mentors are determined in equal measure by the positive and negative influences on us during our own training. Those wishing to be effective mentors may want to recall both what they admired and what they disliked about the work of their own mentors. Further, would-be mentors might reflect on the preparation or lack of preparation they received from their mentors as it relates to their own academic life. Helpful questions to consider may include the following:

- How did your mentor demonstrate that she cared for your academic progress?
- How did your mentor model a successful academic life that was both dedicated and well balanced?
- How did your mentor help nurture your passion for your discipline?

WRITING EXERCISE: Make a list of the characteristics you wish to have as a mentor. Also make a list of the characteristics you wish to avoid as a mentor.

Here are some points to cover in initial meetings with new graduate students in piano.:

- What pieces, exercises, and studies did the person study as an undergraduate?
- What pieces and studies is a student interested in working on at the graduate level?
- Who are the composers whose music the student is most passionate about, and why?

- What specific areas of study, research, or performance is a student interested in pursuing at the graduate level?
- Why did the student decide to pursue piano study at the graduate level?

Starting with questions will both help mentors gather information about students and indicate to students that their well-being and their academic progress and interests are at the center of the mentoring relationship. Mentors also may want to inform students about a number of their own academic and creative pursuits and how those pursuits might intersect with students' interests, offering the following:

- Suggestions about which courses students should take in graduate school
- Advice about which professors students should work with in classes (and which professors they might consider steering clear of!)
- Advice about conferences and meetings that students should consider attending
- Initial advice about potential lines of research to pursue and how the mentor's own research pursuits might assist and complement the student's work

Furthermore, the professor of piano, when acting as a mentor, should create excitement and a sense of wonder and possibility in their students in initial meetings. Typically, studying piano at the graduate level requires extended and often lonely hours in a practice room. Communicating inspiration and a sense of belief in a student's potential will give the student a sense that it will be possible to reach his or her goals as a budding scholar, performer, and professional.

SUPPORTING GRADUATE STUDENTS

The challenges that first-year graduate students in piano face are enormous. Students are often adjusting not only to a new teacher but also a new university, unfamiliar peers, a new geographic location, and a new schooling format. If they are fortunate enough to work as graduate assistants or teaching assistants or are working as accompanists in studios as part of a scholarship assignment, they are facing an additional layer of responsibility and stress. Because of the combination of these particular pressures, nurturing a relationship with a first-year student is critical in the creation of a functioning mentoring relationship during the career of a graduate student.

The formats of undergraduate and graduate education could not be more different. Undergraduate coursework typically features multiple grading milestones over the course of a semester, short-term goals, and a highly structured instructional paradigm. To the newcomer, graduate school may feel unstructured and open-ended. In the context of piano teaching, some graduate programs may not require performance juries and hearings as frequently as undergraduate programs do. All of this means that mentors need to be concrete in their expectations, initially very focused on short-term goals with students, and may benefit from assigning appropriate and specific deadlines for clearly delineated assignments and repertoire.

As graduate students in piano improve in their skills at juggling the many pressures of a graduate education, mentors may consider focusing on the higher-level skills of improving research presentation and communication skills, fostering networking opportunities, and increasing opportunities for presenting at conferences and performing as an artist. For example, master's students in piano performance or pedagogy may be encouraged to submit proposals to statewide piano teachers' meeting or national conferences such as those of the Music Teachers National Association or the National Conference on Keyboard Pedagogy, both of which offer opportunities for students to present. In addition, more advanced students may be encouraged to submit articles about research and practice to journals such as *American Music Teacher* or the *Music Teachers National Association E-Journal*. These types of assignments, which may significantly advance the career of a well-prepared student, may even be integrated into a graduate curriculum. At Michigan State University, I require all second-year master's students in piano pedagogy to submit a proposal to either the Music Teachers National Association or the National Conference on Keyboard Pedagogy, on their own or with the assistance of a select group of peers. I have found that this type of focused higher-level work, when done in conjunction with a thesis project and final recital in the second year, provides concrete benchmarks, opportunities for motivation and achievement, and career advancement to students who participate in it.

ASSISTANCE BEYOND THE DEGREE: LIFELONG MENTORING

After completing graduate work, should a student have the good fortune to secure a teaching position in an institution of higher learning, the process of learning and being mentored should not end. In many ways, the life of a junior faculty member is a natural extension of the graduate school years. The tasks encountered in most early academic careers are very similar to those of graduate school, with natural expansions. Junior faculty teach, as they may have done to varying extents during graduate study. They usually continue to play, now performing solo repertoire and chamber music with colleagues, and sometimes accompanying students. In order to satisfy requirements for reappointment, tenure, and promotion they must meet deadlines, a familiar practice to those used to submitting papers on time, playing juries and recitals, and submitting thesis and dissertation proposals and drafts. To my mind, the significant difference is the lack of standardized mentoring and support among institutions. Some institutions offer dedicated and systematized one-to-one mentoring with a senior faculty member, as well as workshops and continuing education opportunities for faculty in the areas of teaching and learning, research, and work-life balance, whereas some institutions are still wrestling with the question of how to support their faculty in these ways.

Therefore, the role of the mentor as a lifelong supporter is critical. The faculty mentor, as someone who has learned a great deal on the job as it relates to surviving and thriving in an academic position, can offer a great service to former students by remaining in close contact and offering his or her continued service as a regular sounding board for difficult professional decisions, tenure and promotion materials, and personal friendship. In addition, the mentor can provide professional opportunities to former mentees by facilitating performances, masterclasses, and presentations. The mentor's network of professional connections can be offered to the mentee as a "Rolodex" of opportunities and acquaintances that may take a junior faculty member years to gather on his or her own. These services can provide a kick-start to a new faculty member's career that simply may not be possible through other avenues.

A phenomenon that has garnered quite a bit of discussion in academic circles in recent years is that of "imposter syndrome." The phrase describes individuals who are marked by an inability to internalize their accomplishments and a persistent fear of being exposed as a "fraud."[2] Despite external evidence, individuals who exhibit imposter syndrome remain convinced that they do not deserve the success they have achieved. They dismiss their success as being due to luck, timing, or an ability to deceive others into thinking they are more intelligent and competent that they believe themselves to be. This problem has been found to effect men and women almost equally and is somewhat common among early-career professors, for good reason. Being thrust into a teaching position places a lifelong student in the role of teacher and influencer almost immediately, providing a sort of role whiplash that may generate feelings related to lack of worth and substance.

Although imposter syndrome is a serious psychological condition that should be addressed by means of professional counseling and nurturing from a number of different angles, the mentor can do a great deal to avert the formation of this disorder. For one thing, a mentor can provide opportunities for achievement for graduate students that create a healthy sense of success attribution. For example, when a student has a presentation or paper accepted at a conference, a mentor can recognize this success before the student's peers. Perhaps more important, the lifelong mentor can provide a venue for a mentee to voice feelings of fraudulence. Having such an outlet is tremendously important for someone experiencing imposter syndrome, and the listener should be a safe person unconnected to political decisions that may affect a mentee's career. Voicing feelings of fraudulence to a senior faculty member whom the mentee does not trust with confidential information may be harmful to his or her career trajectory.

WRITING EXERCISE: List the competencies you would want your graduates of a two-year master's degree to have. What coursework, research, and performance experience would you provide to your students in order to facilitate achieving them?

Compare your description to the curricula of three master's programs in piano pedagogy that you admire.

MENTORING GRADUATE STUDENTS IN A DIVERSE ACADEMY

Fortunately, most colleges and universities are rich pools of diversity, and ever-increasingly so. A growing number of students come from outside the United States because it continues to be a worldwide leader in higher education, but, perhaps even more encouraging, students today represent a larger number of demographic backgrounds. Graduate programs often proactively seek to attract students who traditionally have been underserved, whether through informal recruitment initiatives or more formal programs such as affirmative action that attempt to address generations of inequality. Furthermore, LGBT students, students who have children, and students with disabilities add to the wonderful mix of classifications of our pupils that creates a more diverse milieu. This varied makeup should force us to reimagine how we deliver our curriculum in refreshing and exciting ways. First and foremost, students from a previously underrepresented group may feel continuously underrepresented and poorly served if there are not professors in their department who come from a similar background. This is perhaps the most important reason why members of twenty-first-century music departments should increase their efforts to recruit faculty from increasingly more diverse backgrounds.

Students from traditionally underrepresented groups may feel isolated from other students in a department if they are among just a few people from a similar background. In departments where I have studied or taught, a large majority of the students have been from Asian backgrounds, with many identifying as international students. This may appear to a newcomer to seem a homogeneous group, but students from various countries may form cliques or more formal communities limited to those from their homeland. This poses challenges if you are the one student from Japan in a department whose members are mainly from the People's Republic of China. Mentors may consider proactively assisting students who feel isolated by introducing them to a diverse range of students in their department, by connecting them with groups on campus or in the community from their specific background, or by addressing their sense of loneliness with sincere attention and care that may occasionally go above and beyond normal duties.

Students from underrepresented groups may not be as active and outgoing in the classroom or studio setting. Be aware of majority-group students' dominating discussions and performance opportunities in classes and studio situations and seek to have less traditionally prominent voices heard more clearly. This sort of proactive engagement will not only benefit minority students, but it will also improve the diversity of viewpoints for all students, leading to a richer mix of frames of reference for all.

The reality of our profession is that tenure-track positions are more and more hard to come by. This, coupled with the fact that graduate programs in piano performance, collaborative piano, and piano pedagogy seem to be more heavily populated each year, means that the role of the mentor is perhaps more crucial to a student's professional success than ever before. The mentoring partnership can better set up a student for a life in the professoriate, this relationship can also be one in which opportunities outside academia are shared, encouraged, and fostered. Teaching of piano by qualified students trained at the graduate level is a sought-after vocation that can take many forms. A mentor who operates in a state of denial about the variety of opportunities available to a performing artist or piano teacher while naively limiting the scope of a career to the academy does not help his or her students in the ever-changing marketplace of opportunities for pianists. The addition of entrepreneurial techniques and a "gigging" skill set will assist students by providing them with the breadth of abilities necessary in the arts economy of the twenty-first century. Coupling this dose of reality with inspiration through the modeling of a life in music and carefully constructed curricula can make the mentoring relationship one of the most beneficial in the career of a graduate student and one of the most gratifying in the life of a professor.

NOTES

1. Hilde de Ridder-Symoens, *A History of the University in Europe*, vol. 1, *Universities in the Middle Ages* (Cambridge: Cambridge University Press, 2003).
2. John Kolligian Jr. and Robert J. Sternberg, "Perceived Fraudulence in Young Adults: Is There an 'Imposter Syndrome'?" *Journal of Personality Assessment* 56, no. 2 (1991): 308–326.

Chapter 10

Working with International Student Pianists

The increased internationalization of our world, and specifically, universities, provides challenges and opportunities for educators. Piano study is no exception, with students from around the globe studying at all levels and in all styles. Further, the very idea of internationalization forces educators, especially piano teachers, to face large philosophical questions about the value of a this type of education. The rapid expansion of international education that has occurred since early in the twenty-first century has created new discussions about the overall issue of international students in higher education. As this expansion of has taken place, and experts have had an opportunity to analyze its effect on institutions, it has become clear that the mere presence of foreign students at a university does not instantly change curriculum and teaching. Yet institutions that implement proactive initiatives in this area have demonstrated more successful outcomes. This development is now a front-and-center issue for university administrations and stakeholders, who now go so far as to feature the concept of the international experience in mission statements. In those excerpted below, the emphasis is mine.

At Michigan State University, the concept of global learning appears in the three main bullet points, which is notable when one considers the preceding line about the university's land-grant heritage: "As a public, research-intensive, land-grant university funded in part by the state of Michigan, our mission is to advance knowledge and transform lives by:

- providing outstanding undergraduate, graduate, and professional education to promising, qualified students in order to prepare them to contribute fully to society as **globally engaged citizen leaders**
- conducting research of the highest caliber that seeks to answer questions and create solutions in order to expand human understanding and make a positive difference, **both locally and globally**
- advancing outreach, engagement, and economic development activities that are innovative, research-driven, and lead to a better quality of life for individuals and communities, **at home and around the world**."[1]

At the University of Southern California, the concept of internationalization has its own prominent paragraph in a lengthy seven-paragraph mission statement:

USC is pluralistic, welcoming outstanding men and women of every race, creed and background. **We are a global institution in a global center, attracting more international students over the years than any other American university.** And we are private, unfettered by political control, strongly committed to academic freedom, and proud of our entrepreneurial heritage.[2]

Columbia University, one of the most prestigious universities in the United States and a member of the famed Ivy League, has the following mission statement:

> Columbia University is one of the world's most important centers of research and at the same time a distinctive and distinguished learning environment for undergraduate and graduate students in many scholarly and professional fields. The University recognizes the importance of its location in New York City and seeks to link its research and teaching to the vast resources of a great metropolis. **It seeks to attract a diverse and international faculty and student body, to support research and teaching on global issues, and to create academic relationships with many countries and regions.** It expects all areas of the university to advance knowledge and learning at the highest level and to convey the products of its efforts to the world.[3]

In addition to these highly public displays of dedication to the education of international students, discussions are taking place about the impact of changing pedagogies on these learners. Similar conversations have begun to occur regarding long-held educational traditions and Western cultural dominance in the current climate of an unprecedented global movement of professors and students, as well as an increasingly fluid exchange of intellectual property and concepts.

In many institutions, including the one where I teach, international students are no longer a minority group in the classroom, rehearsal studio, or private teaching space. Many colleges and conservatories have instituted joint programs with universities in other countries or branch campuses in foreign nations. The rapid expansion of this type of exchange requires that all teachers in such a context quickly re-examine the way they view intellectual tradition, because the global flow of people and ideas seems to be increasing at an exponential rate. This may mean that labeling students simply as "international" is no longer helpful in differentiating their needs from those of other students. Furthermore, such a labeling may lead to a type of segregation of scholars rather than forcing institutions and educators to be dynamic when trying to find new ways of educating and thinking. With online teaching, for example, nationality may become less of an issue. When professors travel to foreign countries to teach, the tables are often turned, as they may themselves become the cultural outsiders. As the presence and diversity of international students continue to rise, major debates are needed regarding English as the primary language, the dominance of the Anglo-American model of higher education, and even American academic imperialism.

Although the traditional flow of international students has been from foreign countries into American universities, the direction of that flow has begun to change. The dynamism and quantity of this flow have perhaps caused increased competition in the international education market as universities in all corners of the globe pursue internationalization of their curriculum and invest in recruitment of foreign students, academic exchange programs, cross-border research collaborations, and joint academic programs. Countries in Europe, Asia, and the Middle East are aggressively expanding their international education programs. The People's Republic of China now accepts more international students than it sends abroad and plans to attract half a million foreign students by the year 2020.[4] The concept of the "brain drain," that is, students only moving from developing to developed countries, is turning into a mutual exchange that is in many cases bidirectional and increasingly equitable. This dynamic circulation means that educators and administrators must consider new strategies and pedagogies for foreign students and native students, who are being thrust into interactions with one another. Cynics may view these developments as merely vehicles for economic expansion; however, universities defend such programs as new ways to share knowledge, foster global understanding and cooperation, and equip students in the home country to compete in an increasingly globalized world.

The expansion of internationalization in the university curriculum obviously changes the demographics within classes, cohorts, and music studios, but it also changes the overall demographics across campuses and within cities and towns where universities reside. Clearly, this mimicking of the increasingly globalized world has the potential to better prepare students and faculty for the professional world they will encounter. When steps are taken to improve and further develop the intercultural skills of all students and faculty, such globalization efforts can have great rewards.

DESIGNING INSTRUCTION FOR INTERNATIONAL STUDENTS

Course design and private instructional design require instructors to engage students' prior knowledge and skills in order to effectively build on that knowledge. While the diversity of students in an internationalized student body presents challenges, it also creates a rich milieu for learning. It is important to attempt to bridge differences in cultural knowledge in order to create a classroom where an international background does not become a disadvantage or even a liability for a student. When approaching work with a foreign student, one should not assume knowledge of home country history and cultural references. An example of this from my own work is the first lesson I taught to a student from the People's Republic of China. Our work on the Three Preludes by Gershwin naturally resulted in a discussion of the origins and stylistic distinctiveness of the blues. After a brief discussion, it was clear that the student had no knowledge of African slavery in the western world. Shocked at first because this topic occupies such a large part of the American psyche, I stopped to consider just how much I knew about Chinese cultural history (very little). What ensued was a fascinating discussion of perhaps the most important topic in American history that allowed her performance to be informed by its cultural situation.

A teacher should also know that skills learned in high schools abroad may not match those expected by teachers used to working with students from the U.S. Some foreign high schools may be more advanced, and others may be less so. This is a particularly important topic to consider for piano teachers working with students from Asian cultures. Although some Asian cultures are perceived as being monolithic with regard to enthusiasm for and extraordinary skill on the piano, the reality is quite a bit more varied, with subtle and not-so-subtle differences in the quality of instruction available, particularly for students from China early in their study. As is the case with students from any culture, early training varies, and this must be taken into account when attempting to design instruction. Classrooms and teaching studios in the U.S. are increasingly interactive spaces, with concepts similar to the "flipped classroom" seeing increased usage. These types of participatory spaces may be quite unfamiliar to international students.

Proven strategies exist for bridging these differences in background knowledge. A strategy that is particularly effective for students of all national backgrounds is being explicit about the extent to which students need to absorb material. Moreover, teachers can incorporate checks for understanding into their classroom and studio presentation style. These types of checks could include the following.

- Asking a student to paraphrase ideas you have presented, or put them in their own words. In the context of a lesson, this could include a question-based mode of introducing new repertoire. "What can you tell me about Beethoven's use of sonata form?" "What does it mean that Debussy's music may be described as Impressionistic?"
- Checking in with students during a lesson by asking, "What questions do you have?" Phrasing the question in this way lets students know that you expect that they will not completely understand a new concept. Stating, "Do you have questions?" implies that a lack of understanding may be unusual.
- In a classroom, asking students to write down names, events, or other specific references that they are not familiar with, in order to clarify them later. Writing them down and even submitting them anonymously may allow the effect of peer pressure or embarrassment to be avoided.
- Make an online chat space available for students to ask and answer questions that may come up owing to unfamiliar material or concepts. These types of spaces are often made available through services like "Blackboard," which are often run and hosted by universities, or can be created in something as simple as a Facebook group.

In general, and as is good practice for the teaching of both foreign and domestic students, providing specific and easy-to-understand instructions about all classroom policies, assignments, and grading rubrics is fundamental. Make it clear that students are welcome to, and expected to, ask questions when they do not understand. In addition, when possible, make it clear that you value differences in student experience and previous training. For example, students from certain countries may not have the technical training that students from other countries may have, simply as a result of the piano training traditions of their home country. An instructor who is aware of these possibilities will be ready for gaps in knowledge and skill, and rather than becoming frustrated, should view them as opportunities for review for all students, as well as possibilities for collaboration and rich discussion.

English proficiency requirements for international students are found in nearly all institutions of higher learning in English-speaking countries, but accommodations and adjustments for non-native speakers of English can make a teacher's instruction even more powerful. Such students will likely fall behind in class participation, especially in the first few weeks of class. A period of adjustment may be required for students who are encountering a class or lesson in English for the first time. Complex academic writing and reading may take noticeably more time for such students. It may be tempting to assign a generous number of readings, but these types of assignments may be a particular challenge to international students. Assigning students to reading and study groups made up of pupils from various backgrounds may provide international students with an opportunity to learn study skills from readers and writers of English, while providing domestic students the opportunity to learn sensitivity to the educational challenges of an international student and develop pedagogical skills in a real-world setting. Delivering a fast-paced lecture may make effective note taking difficult for all students, but especially non-native speakers of English. Providing notes or PowerPoint slides in advance of a lecture can assist all students, regardless of English proficiency, with understanding new material and organizing their notes. Moreover, slowing the pace of the lecture allows time for note taking, as well as room for comprehension checks.

Other strategies for assisting non-native speakers of English might include starting each lecture or lesson with a brief review of the previous lecture or lesson or review of the overarching educational goals of the entire course or semester of lessons. It may also be useful to provide students with an agenda or outline for each class or lesson. When working with an international student in a piano lesson, it may be useful to give the student an assignment or homework sheet with clear expectations about what should be prepared for the next lesson.

Below is a sample assignment sheet.

Prepare for February 14:
All major scales and arpeggios, 4 octaves, hands together, parallel motion (I will grade your performance on three of these scales, of my choosing)
Beethoven Sonata op. 31, no. 2: please perform the first movement by memory. Hands apart practice is essential.

Upcoming Goals:
All major and minor scales and arpeggios (learned by Spring Break)
Beethoven Sonata, all movements (memorized by Spring Break)
Perform Beethoven Sonata by memory in the last studio class in March

When teaching a large lecture course using PowerPoint slides, posting these slides online may be helpful, particularly for students whose first language is not English. The ability to preview these slides before a lecture may prime students for the concepts they may encounter in the coming lecture, while helping smooth over difficulties in difficult-to-grasp grammar and vocabulary. The ability to review these slides soon after a lecture may help students cement complex new concepts and allow them to look up the definitions of words they did not know on first hearing. Providing opportunities to use such building blocks for a new or less-familiar language can allow foreign students to improve English skills as well as learn subject.

In order to improve the interactive nature of a piano lesson and to increase student participation, encourage students to submit questions via email about their music in advance of a lesson. This tactic has numerous advantages for an international student: writing a question, as well as asking it, forces a student to grapple with both written and spoken English, necessary skills for working professionally in an English-speaking country. This practice also demonstrates to students that their questions are valued and are being listened to closely by their teacher. It gives the teacher an all-too-rare opportunity to prepare specifics in advance of a lesson. Such a policy creates a situation in which the student-teacher dynamic is an exchange, cultivating, it is hoped, an environment where instruction is more effectively received and where students feel as if their goals and opinions are valued and are being taken into consideration by a teacher when a curriculum is crafted.

The creation of a buddy system or a more formal group teaching and practicing system can encourage students to rely on their colleagues' expertise and knowledge when outside the instructional space. Within a piano studio, pairing up students as "accountability partners" can be a powerful tool, especially when a native student is paired with an international one, to the advantage of both. The opportunity to get to know a student from the home country may give a foreign student a community within which to build confidence. The chance to practice English conversation with a native English speaker can be powerful. It is an understandable impulse of international students to associate closely with students from their country. Pairing an international student with a native student can at once battle this natural impulse and supplement it, providing diversity to a student's experience while studying in a foreign country.

Such a pairing would also have advantages for the native student. Befriending and working closely with a student from a foreign country has the potential to create empathy in the native student for the experience of the international student. Challenges of relocation, language, and distance from family and friends can be relayed effectively to a native student in a situation like this. Native students may also learn about new ways to think and study from nonnative peers. In piano teaching, it is generally accepted that students from Asian countries typically have a discipline of practicing that exceeds that of American students. Encountering such diligence can widen the viewpoint of a native student and create inspiration and excitement. Moreover, the opportunity to learn deeply about another student's culture can create a powerful new experience for a native student. In an increasingly globalized educational and professional world, these types of experiences are becoming more and more necessary.

Differences in English-language fluency may lead instructors to finish sentences or words for non-native speakers, rather than taking the time to listen to the complete thought. It is important for instructors to show care and genuine empathy for their students, and one way to show this is by listening deeply and completely. Not only does this type of listening exhibit to a student patience and empathy on the part of an instructor, but it also, in the long term, may cause an instructor to better understand the cadences and unique features of a speech from a particular region of the world.

The two-way nature of verbal communication makes it critical for instructors in an internationalized educational setting to improve their ability to understand non-native speakers while assisting them with their English skills.

An instructor in the United States may be accustomed to using American phrases, including humor, idioms, and slang, in order to invigorate or lighten the mood of a lecture or to demonstrate to students his or her awareness of popular culture specific to the age group being taught. Although it may be useful or important for international students to eventually understand these phrases, they may initially exclude foreign students. When informal or slang phrases are used, it is important to provide a way for any student to inquire about what they mean. In a private lesson, this may be a short conversation. In a classroom setting, students may be encouraged to communicate with a professor or a teaching assistant about them outside of class. Also, instructors should be aware of the pace of their speech and cultural references that they may take for granted. For example, basic references to American cultural history may be lost on an international student.

Everyone operates with a certain level of bias. An example of a type of bias that can be particularly dangerous when working with international students is stereotyping of national styles and characters. In the world of piano teaching, it is easy to characterize students from Asian countries in ways that ignore their individuality. The attitudes and work ethics of students from a similar national background are never uniform. Some frequently encountered preconceived ideas about international students may include the belief that they lack the individualism and independence of learning found in students from the United States. A notion that is more specific to music that also is not necessarily true is that students from Asian countries value technical proficiency over emotion in their performances. In my extensive work with students from Asian countries I have seen that this type of generalization could not be farther from the truth. When instructors paint with these types of broad brush strokes, they may not search for the type of personally crafted instruction that is required for reaching any individual.

> **WRITING EXERCISE: We all engage in stereotyping. Answer the following questions to consider how you engage in stereotyping:**
> All wealthy students are _____
> All American students are _____
> All students from China are _____
> While ideally you found these prompts impossible to complete, it is hoped that this exercise helped you consider your own attitudes. What other prompts would you consider including in an exercise like this? What stereotypes would you like to eliminate from your mind before you engage in the teaching of international students?

Ultimately, the presence of international students in the classroom or teaching studio is a valuable asset for an instructor attuned to the richness of their presence. Giving native students opportunities to learn about various cultural perspectives is a built-in educational dividend. If an instructor takes the time to effectively address national stereotypes in a way that supplements and enriches curricular content, the scope and understanding of a student's place in an increasingly connected world can be improved. If a student is then able to apply such knowledge to experiences and interactions outside the classroom, then discussion of the nature of national stereotypes is instructional time well spent.

ACADEMIC INTEGRITY AND THE INTERNATIONAL STUDENT

Academic integrity among international students is perhaps the most challenging and frequently encountered topic in working with diverse populations. Much of this concern revolves around plagiarism. The practice is frequently encountered with American university students as well, but there are a number of circumstances specific to the experience of international students that are critical for instructors to know and understand. The fundamental point of departure for many situations regarding plagiarism and international students is that the Western custom of citation of sources is not at all universal. In many East Asian educational systems, it is normal to directly use information from a book or professor verbatim and without citation. This type of usage is even viewed as a sign of respect. In addition, students from collectivist cultures may view knowledge as a pursuit done together, and therefore usage without citation may have an entirely different meaning. Language difficulties may also preclude students from fully understanding codes of conduct. It may be useful to include a code of conduct exam with your syllabus to diagnose whether students of both international and native backgrounds are able to understand and apply the rules.

While the importance of enforcing and maintaining an academic code of conduct cannot be underestimated, as mentioned above, there is no global standard for academic integrity. Instructors should understand the reasons why, so as to gain context for possible infractions by international students, in order to see the educational experience through their eyes. One of the underlying factors that may lead to an international student running afoul of a school's code of conduct is a language barrier, which may make it difficult for international students to understand a policy and know how to implement it. Also, the concept of "common knowledge" may be fluid when viewed through the lenses of different cultures. "Common knowledge" is matter known by nearly everyone in a particular field or community. As it relates to academic pursuits, it is typically not considered information that needs to be cited. What is common knowledge to someone from an African country may not be common knowledge from someone from a North American country. Thus, citation becomes a particularly challenging topic.

Cheating in some form is considered to be wrong in all cultures; however, ideas about collaboration and how it interfaces with cheating may differ widely from one culture to another. Many students, and in particular, international students, may believe that the professor is the ultimate authority in the classroom and even in larger and more important venues. In some Asians countries, the importance of the professor is much greater than in the United States. With this in mind, teachers should understand that they provide the most powerful and effective guidance for students when it comes to academic integrity and that this information should not simply come an academic integrity website or brochure. Using initial violations of academic integrity as learning experiences can provide significant clarifications that can serve as the initial stages of a scaffolding that students can build on throughout their academic career. While nipping small infractions in the bud is important so as not to create larger, more harmful episodes later on, reinforcing and reminding students about expectations of academic honesty prior to large examinations and term papers is also critical for all students.

The teaching of international students is both satisfying and necessary work in the modern academy. Quickly and effectively getting up to speed with best practices in this type of teaching can assist a professor to navigate these increasingly important waters.

NOTES

1. Michigan State University, Office of the President, "MSU Mission Statement." Accessed April 19, 2017. http://president.msu.edu/advancing-msu/msu-mission-statement.html.
2. University of Southern California, "About USC." Accessed April 19, 2017. https://about.usc.edu/policies/mission-statement/.
3. Columbia University, "Mission Statement." Accessed April 19, 2017. http://www.columbia.edu/content/mission-statement.html.
4. "Brains without borders," *Economist*, January 30, 2016. Accessed March 5, 2017. http://www.economist.com/news/international/21689540-australia-and-canada-seek-attract-more-foreign-students-america-and-britain-could.

Chapter 11

What Can We Learn from Some of History's Great Piano Teachers?

The instrument we teach has been in existence for more than three hundred years. Bartolomeo Cristofori was a harpsichord maker based in Florence who invented the "fortepiano" around the turn of the eighteenth century. The first official record of a piano appears in an inventory of the holdings of the Medici family, who were sponsors of Cristofori, dated 1700. The only surviving Cristofori instruments date from the 1720s, the general time at which he ceased experimentation and development of the fortepiano.[1] The fortepiano was a significant departure from the harpsichord and other keyboard instruments in that its action was a completely new invention. Rather than plucking the strings, as on the harpsichord, or touching the strings, as on the clavichord, the player struck the strings on the fortepiano, allowing both a freer ringing tone as a result of the percussive nature of sound production and tonal gradation by way of touch, not previously available to performers to any great degree on other keyboard instruments. In addition, the Cristofori fortepiano utilized stronger and tenser strings that were attached to a frame that was significantly more massive than harpsichords of the day. Cristofori also included a soft pedal, which caused the hammers to strike fewer strings, much as the modern una corda pedal does. Cristofori essentially created a new instrument from the ground up that was only tangentially related to previous keyboard instruments. With this new invention came a brand-new repertoire, new demands on the performer, and a fresh school of piano teaching that eventually became what we know today as the field of piano pedagogy.

CARL PHILIPP EMANUEL BACH

Perhaps the first great champion of the music and pedagogical aspects of the fortepiano was Carl Philipp Emanuel Bach, the second son of Johann Sebastian Bach (see figure 11.1). Carl Philipp Emanuel Bach was a noted performer, composer of works in a new style following the death of his father, and important contributor to pedagogy to whom we still owe a great deal. His *Essay on the True Art of Playing Keyboard Instruments* remains a profound and exhaustive volume covering a range of topics related to piano pedagogy and performance including technical, stylistic, and artistic topics, as well as a sort of textbook for learning the art of continuo playing. Clementi wrote of the *Essay on the True Art,* "Whatever I know of fingering and the new style, in short, whatever I understand of the pianoforte I learned from this book,"[2] Johann Sebastian Bach was decidedly naïve about the pianoforte; however, Carl Philipp Emanuel was quite familiar with this new instrument. Apparently he was not an artist of the same technical prowess as his father, Scarlatti, or Handel. He was, however, considered to be one of the most expressive, artistic, and sensitive keyboard players of his day. Part of what we owe to C. P. E. Bach is his attention to both artistic and technical matters in the *Essay.* The book is a compendium of basically all that was known about playing keyboard instruments up

Fig. 11.1. Engraving of Carl Philipp Emanuel Bach, 1816, by Heinrich Eduard Winter (1788–1829)

to his day. Bach established rules regarding improvisation, figured bass, accompaniment, performance practice, embellishments, and fingerings in the *Essay*. His suggestions regarding fingering for scales essentially created the systems of fingering that we still follow today. Bach recommended that a keyboard musician play with arched fingers and relaxed muscles throughout the arms.

Bach's instructions about musical interpretation greatly influenced performance in the impending classical era. Bach spends a significant amount of space in the *Essay* on developing taste in a musician. In the eighteenth century, the concept of taste centered quite strongly on the ability of the performer to place his or her personal stamp on a performance, particularly in the realms of style and technique. Bach's advice regarding taste deals with concepts of the limits and application of tempo rubato, the ability of the pianist to imitate the expressive capabilities of the human voice, and the tasteful use of embellishments. Moreover, in a plea on behalf of performers and pedagogues alike, Bach encouraged composers to notate their music with more specific markings indicating more specific ornamentation, tempo markings, and expressive terms whenever possible. Bach believed that employing these tactics would clarify the message of a composer's music.

WOLFGANG AMADEUS MOZART

The very concept of stand-alone piano lessons was quite uncommon during the late eighteenth century. In a letter to his mother dated February 7, 1778, Wolfgang Amadeus Mozart stated quite firmly the following about piano teaching: "I leave that to people who cannot do anything but play the piano. I am a composer."[3] In Mozart's day, vocal or instrumental instruction was not typically taught in isolation but was paired with significant and often evenly weighted instruction in music theory and composition. Despite his apparent aversion to piano teaching, Mozart still had numerous keyboard students who greatly affected his work as a composer of fortepiano music. The Concerto in C, K. 238, was dedicated to the Salzburg countess Antonia Lützow in 1776. The Sonata in C, K. 309, was dedicated to his student Rosa Cannabich. During the last decade of Mozart's life in Vienna, his teaching increased significantly. Perhaps this lucrative pursuit was born out of necessity because of his newfound life as a freelance artist after the relative financial and professional stability of his earlier years under the patronage of the

Archbishop of Salzburg. In a letter to his father from January 1782, Mozart wrote: "I have three pupils now.... I no longer charge for twelve lessons, but monthly.... I shall get several more on these terms, but I really need only one more, because four pupils are quite enough" (see figure 11.2).

Mozart typically gave his students three to five one-hour lessons per week. Letters to his father indicate that Mozart preferred to teach during the middle of the day, reserving the early morning and late night for composing. He apparently believed in the establishment of absolute fundamental pianistic technique. In letters to and evaluations of students, he indicated that independence of

Fig. 11.2. Portrait of Wolfgang Amadeus Mozart (*Naumanns Illustrirte Musikgeschichte*, late 1800s)

the fingers in each hand was indispensable, recommending that students practice scales, arpeggios, and passagework on a keyboard covered with a handkerchief or small napkin, believing that such a practice technique would expose even the smallest imperfections in terms of evenness of touch. The only technical exercise we know of by Mozart stresses finger independence through the practicing of broken chords. Mozart's students were a varied and influential group. Perhaps his most unusual student was Prince Karl Lichnowsky, who was both Mozart's student and patron. Lichnowsky financed Mozart's trips to Berlin, Leipzig, Dresden, and Prague and facilitated living arrangements for a young Beethoven in 1792.[4] Beethoven's first residence in Vienna was at one of Lichnowsky's homes. Furthermore, Lichnowsky assisted Beethoven with a concert tour in 1796. Beethoven admired Lichnowsky greatly and dedicated his op. 1, three piano trios, and the Sonata op. 13 to the prince. Thus, one of Mozart's students served as an important figure in the patronage of two of the giants of classical music. Who in our own piano studios might have the passion and connections to serve as a modern-day Prince Karl Lichnowsky? The passion and love that we instill in our students may manifest itself in the future in astonishing ways. Teachers should seek to nurture these aspects of our students in order to potentially preserve the art form itself.

    Mozart served as an instructor of harmony and piano to Barbara Ployer, who was apparently one of his favorite students. Two of his most enduring piano concertos, K. 449 and K. 453, were dedicated to Ployer. She kept a notebook that outlines exercises in four-part harmony for string quartet, four-part harmony for keyboard, and occasionally but much more infrequently, contrapuntal textures. Two additional student notebooks from the 1780s exist that contain information about compositional and pianistic material that Mozart covered in lessons.[5] Thomas Attwood, an English composer, and

Franz Jakob Freystädtler, a young German composer and pianist, studied concurrently with Mozart, most likely from 1786 to 1787.[6] It is clear from letters that he considered these two young men to be colleagues rather than just students, and both became his close friends. Despite Mozart's admiration for the work of these men, their notebooks indicate that Mozart had them study rudimentary elements of composition and keyboard, building their basic technical skills from the ground up.

CARL CZERNY

Carl Czerny, an Austrian pianist, teacher, and composer, was born in 1791 and died in 1857. Czerny stands alone in terms of his prolific output of technical studies, which are still widely used today. He began teaching at the age of fifteen, basing his teaching method on the traditions established by Beethoven and Muzio Clementi. Czerny encountered Franz Liszt for the first time in 1819. Czerny recalled Liszt's playing in this meeting as follows: "He was a pale, sickly-looking child, who, while playing, swayed about on the stool as if drunk. His playing was irregular, untidy, confused, and he threw his fingers quite arbitrarily all over the keyboard. But that notwithstanding, I was astonished at the talent Nature had bestowed upon him."[7]

Czerny was, early on, so taken by the young Liszt's pianistic potential that he taught him free of charge. Liszt became Czerny's most famous pupil. After 1840, Czerny taught very infrequently and devoted himself almost exclusively to composition. As a tribute to his teacher, Liszt dedicated his Transcendental Etudes to Czerny.

Czerny is considered widely to be the developer of modern piano technique. Because many of his students became tremendously influential teachers as part of their professional profile, including Theodor Kullak, Franz Liszt and Theodor Leschetizky, an astonishing number of contemporary pianists and piano teachers can trace their teaching lineage to Czerny (including the author of this book). The music magazine *The Etude* published a chart illustrating Czerny's influence among pianists by 1927 (see figure 11.3).

Influential lineages reaching back to the teaching of Czerny include Wanda Landowska (a student of Moritz Moszkowski, who was a student of Theodor Kullak), Sergei Prokofiev (a student of Anna Yesipova, who was a student of Theodor Leschetizky), Arthur Rubinstein (a student of Ignacy Jan Paderewski, who was a student of Leschetizky), Claudio Arrau (a student of Martin Krause, who was a student of Liszt) and Daniel Barenboim (a student of Edwin Fischer, who was a student of Krause).

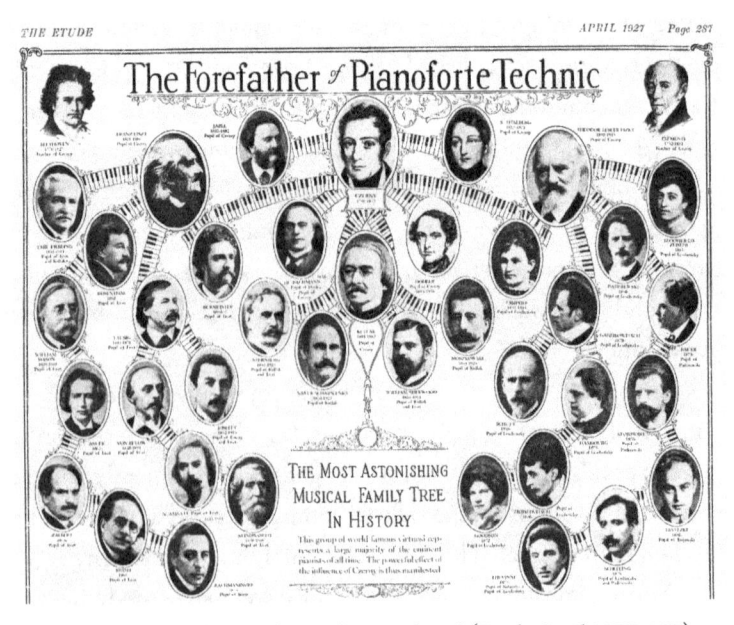

Fig. 11.3. "The Forefather of Pianoforte Technic" (*Etude*, April 1927, 287)

FRANZ LISZT

Franz Liszt, the larger-than-life figure at the heart of nineteenth-century piano performance, literature, and pedagogy, was the most famous and influential of Carl Czerny's students (see figure 11.4). Liszt's influence as a composer and concert artist is legendary, but his work as a piano teacher is just as critical to his output, if not as readily known. Liszt apparently did the bulk of his teaching in the masterclass setting, rather than in private lessons. In these classes he would teach between ten and twenty students at a time. He apparently did not assign specific pieces but allowed students to choose their own repertoire with the agreement that they would ask him what pieces they should prepare for the next class. Liszt's student Arthur Friedheim described Liszt's teaching format as follows: "In his master classes, Liszt would talk about the work being performed, discussing its relation with other music by the same composer, and with previous and contemporary works. He would point out the form and proportions of the piece and its moments of climax. All playing was done from memory, and his pupils practiced six or seven hours a day."[8] Liszt believed fervently in the idea that pianists in training should have the opportunity to perform before audiences. An exceptional student of his, Amy Fay, described a time when she brought a piece to play for Liszt while musical scholars were assembled in his salon. Fay asked the scholars to leave because she was nervous about playing for them, but Liszt insisted that she do so, stating, "Oh, that is healthy for you, you have a choice audience now."[9]

Liszt was a groundbreaking teacher of the piano when one considers how his methodology was essentially a complete break from many previous traditions. His essential goal for all of his students was that they learn to transmit the emotion and character of a work to an audience.[10] Liszt typically did not teach technical fundamentals because all of the students accepted into his studio were expected to have comprehensive technical proficiency. In spite of Liszt's reputation as a technical powerhouse, he was less concerned with the pure technical concerns of teaching than were other notable teachers of the day, including Rudolf Breithaupt, Theodor Kullak, Ludwig Deppe, and Friedrich Kalkbrenner. Many of these gentlemen wrote extensively about the technical approach to the piano, mainly advising very little physical movement and making strict suggestions about posture. Liszt disagreed with many of these philosophies, stating instead that the physical uniqueness

Fig. 11.4. Portrait of Liszt from *Technical Studies for the Pianoforte* by Franz Liszt (J. Schuberth & Co., 1886)

of each student should dictate his or her technical approach to the instrument. In a holistic way he believed in honoring the individualistic impulses of all of his students and believed specifically that it would be folly to create in them clones of himself or of other famous pianists.

Amy Fay wrote frequently about Liszt's demeanor and attitude during lessons, describing lessons as always having a feeling of freedom and liberty. Liszt apparently never wished to impose his personal ideas about interpretation on students. Fay stated, "You feel so free with him, and he develops the very spirit of music in you. He doesn't keep nagging at you all the time, but he leaves you your own conception. Now and then he will make a criticism, or play a passage, and with a few words give you enough to think of all the rest of your life. There is a delicate point to everything he says, as subtle as he is himself. He doesn't tell you anything about the technique. That you must work out for yourself."[11]

Franz Liszt did not accept payment for his piano teaching. While this remarkable situation was made possible by his incredible professional success as a composer and performer, that he taught nearly four hundred students during his career shows that he found teaching to be a valuable and necessary endeavor. Although the competition for a place in Liszt's studio was tremendous, Liszt was a paternal figure with his students, displaying a gentle, polite personal demeanor without a hint of intimidation. In addition to being heavily invested in students' musical development, Liszt was also deeply interested in a students' greater life, including material, spiritual, and emotional matters.

The traditions of Franz Liszt as a teacher are far-reaching and undeniably influential up to the present day. Unfortunately, there is much fascination with Liszt's technical legacy as it relates to piano pedagogy and very little regarding the mentoring relationships he

Fig. 11.5. Liszt and his students (1884) (Liszt and his students, Louis Held, 1884)

established and codified as norms, expectations, and best practices in piano teaching. Furthermore, this lineage of mentoring, as passed down through generations of teachers and pianists, illustrates the tremendous respect through emulation that his own pupils had for their teacher. The serious student of piano pedagogy who may be eager to continue in this great line of instruction should learn extensively about Liszt the mentor, a man to whom we owe a great deal in terms of how to best serve students in this unique and effective relationship between piano teacher and student (see figure 11.5).

JOSEF LHEVINNE

Josef Lhevinne was a pianistic giant in the Russian tradition and a piano teacher of great importance. Together with his wife Rosina

Lhevinne and on his own, Joseph Lhevinne occupies a tremendous sphere of influence in the piano pedagogy traditions of the early twentieth century. A longtime teacher at the Juilliard School, he was regarded as a supreme technician of the piano by nearly every peer. His book about piano playing and teaching, *Basic Principles in Pianoforte Playing*, is a concise volume that describes in clear detail his concept of the essential elements of successful piano playing, including a thorough knowledge of scales, the indispensable use of rests for emotional effect in performance, the essential qualities of rhythm as it relates to all music, the importance of ear training in the developing pianist, and the attainment of a beautiful tone. Lhevinne provides specific musical examples to illustrate a number of these concepts and stresses the idea that technique, though fundamental, must be subservient to an understanding of music, form, and emotion.[12]

ROSINA LHEVINNE

Rosina Lhevinne was in many ways a more influential teacher than her husband. Rosina, five years the junior of Josef, first studied with her future husband at the Moscow Imperial Conservatory, where Josef was a highly regarded student. When they were married, Josef's international concert career was already well under way. Because of this, Rosina decided to selflessly give up her own goal of becoming a concert artist, instead focusing on her output as a teacher and two-piano partner with her husband. The Lhevinnes left Russia and came to New York to teach at the Juilliard School after World War I and the Russian Revolution. For nearly forty-six years Rosina acted as a teacher who prepared students for Josef. Following his death at age seventy, Rosina was granted Josef's full position at the

Juilliard School. Her students included some of the greatest pianists, composers, piano teachers, and conductors of the mid-twentieth century, including James Levine, John Williams, John Browning, Daniel Pollack, Misha Dichter, Edward Auer, and Garrick Ohlsson. Rosina Lhevinne continued to teach at Juilliard and at the University of Southern California in Los Angeles until her death in 1976 at age ninety-six. She perpetuated the great Russian tradition of piano teaching also adhered to by her husband Josef, which included the concepts of complete technical command of all aspects of the instrument (which were nonetheless subservient to exposing the great beauty inherent in canonical compositions as indicated by the composer) and strong individuality.[13]

ADELE MARCUS

Adele Marcus was an American pianist and pedagogue who lived from 1906 to 1995. Born in Kansas City, Marcus studied with Josef Lhevinne and Artur Schnabel, serving for a number of years as Lhevinne's assistant. Marcus was on the piano faculty at the Juilliard School in New York from 1954 to 1990 and gave masterclasses at many other universities and conservatories during her teaching career. She taught many important pianists of the twentieth and twenty-first centuries including Horacio Gutierrez, Byron Janis, Stephen Hough, Panayis Lyras, Jon Kimura Parker, Jeffrey Swann, Norman Krieger, and Santiago Rodriguez.[14] Although Marcus was a remarkable pianist, teaching was the center of her career. She began teaching in 1939, and taught only young children for ten years. Marcus referred to this as the formative period in her teaching career, which helped her develop into the legendary teacher that she eventually became. She served on numerous international competition juries, taught for a time at the Aspen Music Festival, and founded her own summer piano festival in Norway.

As with all teachers, Adele Marcus's influence goes well beyond her ideas about technique. An exponent of the high Romantic school of playing, she was able to transmit exhaustive and complete ideas about interpretation, style, and wit, along with practical advice about concert presentation and a career in music. One of the most lasting legacies of Marcus's teaching is the series of technical exercises she called "Setting up Exercises." Although Marcus insisted that her students already have an assured and strong fundamental technique, she nonetheless prescribed a series of exercises that involved stretching, strength, and independence of fingers that were gleaned from great pianists of her day and the recent past, including Vladimir Horowitz and Sergei Rachmaninoff. These exercises are available in a number of informal transcribed formats online, as well as in videos shared on YouTube by a few of her former students.[15]

LEON FLEISHER

Leon Fleisher is an American pianist, conductor, and piano teacher born in 1928 in San Francisco. Like many of the other great piano teachers mentioned in this chapter, Fleisher was a child prodigy, making his public debut at age eight and his debut with the New York Philharmonic at age sixteen. Fleisher was accepted as a young man into the class of the acclaimed Artur Schnabel, linking his training directly to Beethoven through Carl Czerny and Theodor Leschetizky. In the 1950s, Fleisher made acclaimed and now-iconic recordings of many of the canonical pieces in the piano repertoire, including concerti of Brahms, Beethoven, Mozart, Grieg, and Schumann, as well as the *Symphonic Variations* of Franck and Rachmaninoff's

Rhapsody on a Theme of Paganini. In 1964 Fleisher lost the use of his right hand. At the time, the cause was a mystery. Eventually, his problem was diagnosed as focal dystonia, a neurological condition that affects a group of muscles in a specific part of the body that may cause involuntary muscle contractions or spasms. In the case of Fleisher, focal hand dystonia caused the fingers in his right hand to curl into the palm without control. The causes of focal dystonia are not entirely known. Scientists currently believe that it may be due to a misfiring of neurons in a part of the brain that causes muscular contractions. The misfiring of these neurons essentially eliminates selectivity in how the brain selects muscles to move.[16]

For Fleisher and his admirers, the onset of this condition was tragic. Nonetheless, he performed and recorded nearly all of the left-hand repertoire available and took up conducting during this time. In the 1990s he became able to play with both hands again as a result of his use of experimental Botox injections.

In addition to his trailblazing work as a two-handed and a left-handed pianist and as a conductor, Leon Fleisher is perhaps the most influential and sought-after American piano teacher. He has taught both conducting and piano at the Peabody Institute of the Johns Hopkins University, at the Curtis Institute of Music, at the Royal Conservatory of Music in Toronto, and at the Tanglewood Music Center. His students, including Yefim Bronfman, Kevin Kenner, Louis Lortie, André Watts, Jack Winerock, and Orit Wolf, are among the most important pianists of the twentieth and twenty-first centuries.

Fleisher teaches his students exclusively in a masterclass setting, similar to the environment in which Franz Liszt taught. All members of his studio must attend every lesson taught within the studio and must bring scores of the works being studied. There are multiple advantages to such an arrangement. The piano repertoire, as vast and far-reaching as it is, cannot be learned in its entirety by one person in the span of an average lifetime. Attending the lessons of peers allows a student to learn his or her own repertoire at the same time as everyone else's. Furthermore, the third-person vantage point in a piano lesson can be very enlightening. When, as a student, you are in the throes of performing, understanding and retaining information covered can be quite difficult. The distance afforded to someone who is simply observing a lesson can in and of itself provide an educational advantage.

The connection between music and math is commonly made in pedagogical circles. The similarities between these fields of study are obvious and useful on the surface. Fleisher, however, focuses much of his discussion during a lesson on movement and physics and the way they impact momentum and gravity in music. In Fleisher's studio at the Peabody Institute, images of a soaring bird and photographs of distant nebulae captured by the Hubble Space Telescope are placed on a wall opposite the two Steinway B's. Fleisher states, "They represent a sense of what we aspire to. A sense of space, the sublime, the transcendent."[17] Hours of video of Fleisher's teaching can be watched online at the Leon Fleisher Archive at the Peabody Institute (http://musiclibrary.peabody.jhu.edu/fleisher). This teaching is practical, gentle, completely guided by the needs of the student and the music, and tremendously inspiring. The piano teacher in training will learn a great deal about both the art of teaching and the piano repertoire itself by digesting all of these videos.

RUSSELL SHERMAN

Russell Sherman in an American pianist, teacher, and, based on his tremendous gift with the written word in his series of essays *Piano Pieces*, author. Sherman was born in New York in 1930, and made his debut at the Town Hall at age fifteen. He studied piano with the famed Austro-American pianist and composer Edward Steuermann and composition with Erich Itor Kahn. During his illustrious career Sherman has performed as a soloist with many of the major American symphony orchestras, including the New York Philharmonic, the Los Angeles Philharmonic, the Boston Symphony, the Chicago Symphony and the Philadelphia Orchestra. Sherman's recordings of many of the masterworks for the piano are not only considered iconic, but might also be called iconoclastic. His unique voice is irresistible in his recordings of Beethoven, Chopin, Gershwin, Debussy, and contemporary works, but perhaps most important, his recording of the complete *Transcendental Etudes* by Liszt is still fresh, shocking, and authoritative. I have had the pleasure of hearing Russell Sherman a number of times in recital at Michigan State University, and each performance has been riveting, enrapturing, and electric, even in his now advanced age.

Sherman is currently artist-in-residence at the New England Conservatory. One of his former students, Wha Kyung Byun, is now his wife, and she has also established herself as one of the premier teachers of the instrument. "Miss Byun" is also on the faculty of the New England Conservatory. Sherman has been the teacher of acclaimed artists and teachers around the globe including Christopher O'Riley, Christopher Taylor, Deborah Moriarty, and Norman Krieger.

Sherman's book *Piano Pieces* is a challenging and indispensable collection of short essays published in 1996. In it Sherman writes, "To know the piano is to know the universe. To master the piano is to master the universe." These are, perhaps, the least challenging of all the sentences contained in this volume. The writing is dense, poetic, full of metaphor, and at times quite disconcerting (in the best possible way). This collection is not a light read full of practical advice for the piano teacher in training but, rather, a philosophical tome made to help a student or teacher consider deep truths and untruths about music on multiple readings, over a lifetime.

Russell Sherman is a sort of priest of classical music, seemingly concerned only with teaching and performing the music of the great masters in such a way that it provides an alternate and more beautiful way of examining a sometimes dreadful world. Regarding the appropriation of classical music for entertainment, Sherman states, "No response other than stubborn resistance and fury seems appropriate for me to the many meretricious compromises of the day. And if I vent my anger, it is because music was presented to me as the province of legends, heroes, and saints."[18] *Piano Pieces* is, if nothing else, a thought-provoking and sometimes combative volume that somehow has a way of making the piano teacher feel as if his or her work is of the utmost cultural importance. Each time I read this book, I am both intellectually challenged and emotionally charged. I highly recommend it.

When Gunther Schuller became president of the struggling New England Conservatory in the 1970s he brought Russell Sherman to Boston. Throughout his distinguished teaching career at that school Sherman has particularly encouraged the individuality of students' artistic thumbprint and has frequently lectured about how the insistence on technical perfection on the concert stage is a scourge on classical performance. In addition to teaching a highly select group of students, Sherman is a notorious practicer, working at the piano between seven and eight hours per day. In an interview with the *Boston Globe* he said, "I would confess all of my students have more mechanics than I have. But for me technique is the ability to draw colors and meanings and characters and qualities out of the sound. This technique takes a long, long time to develop. The other stuff, I think, stays in place because I need it to make the colors."[19]

Although this chapter presents only a small sampling of the exceptional teachers of the piano in its relatively short history (at least when compared to other instruments in Western classical music), any teacher can learn a great deal when studying the lives and teaching practices of these legendary instructors.

TECHNIQUE AND MUSIC

All of the piano teachers highlighted in this chapter have a commitment to pushing forward the concepts of technical command and musical idea in both their own teaching practice as well as the field at large. Carl Philipp Emmanuel Bach, perhaps the first major figure in piano pedagogy to codify many of the key aspects of the playing and teaching of the fortepiano, dedicated just as much time to describing, in detail, the specifics of concepts such as scale fingering, the physical approach to the instrument, and basic elements of a healthy and effective technique as he did to musical style, the concept of the pianist's imitating the phrasing and breathing of a singer, and the music theory behind continuo performance on harpsichord. Wolfgang Amadeus Mozart, clearly dedicated to the teaching of musical fundamentals and basics, insisted that even his most advanced students in both piano performance and composition learn technical rudiments. At the same time, Mozart cared for the professional lives of his pupils, treating them as peers and colleagues as he sought to launch their careers by creating opportunities for them to perform with him, give premieres of his works, and encounter musical benefactors who had given him a leg up at some point. Carl Czerny was, perhaps, the teacher who contributed the most to the development of modern piano technique in physical terms. Yet that was not his only contribution to piano pedagogy, as his artistic influence created a lineage of pianists and teachers that has been driving the field forward ever since. Franz Liszt, perhaps most of all, was the paragon of balance when it came to combining elements of virtuoso technical training and musical understanding in his teaching, performance, and compositions. Let us not forget, as well, Russell Sherman's acknowledgment of the importance of his own hours at the instrument and his messages about how technique is subservient to the intentions of a composer.

Great piano teaching, at any level, should not be primarily concerned with technique or artistic training but should be a comprehensive and organic combination of both. We learn from the greatest teachers of our instrument that separating these concepts does not serve the music or the student well and creates a situation wherein musical skills are relegated to a role similar to that of simple athletic skills in sports. Music is an all-encompassing pursuit that touches on all parts of the human experience. We risk extinguishing a student's spark for this great adventure when we focus solely on one aspect of playing at the expense of another.

Perhaps the overarching theme of this book is the power that we have as teachers when we show genuine care for our students based not on our own glory but on their place in the world. This is not a new concept at all. Mozart spoke extensively in letters to his father about both his frustrations and optimism about the approach his students took in their study. Liszt refused to accept tuition for any of his teaching and mentored students in matters related to both their material and spiritual well-being. From the writings of Amy Fay, we see that Liszt understood his almost fatherly role with his students in a way that had enormous impact on all parts of their lives, and furthermore, provided them with immense confidence and purpose. Adele Marcus embodied the idea that students produce effective work when they feel cared for and when they leave a lesson understanding the path and steps they must take to bring their playing to the next level. Her quotations about teaching indicate that her concern was not her own glory but the success and progress of her students on a week-to-week basis.

There exists an unfortunate viewpoint in our field, and in our culture at large, that teaching is a secondary pursuit that should be settled for by those for whom a "more professional" track does not pan out. The greatest weapon against this dangerous and patently untrue opinion is study of the careers of our greatest teachers. Josef Lhevinne, one of the greatest virtuosos of the twentieth century, could have cultivated a lucrative artistic life that consisted solely of performance. His dedication to training the next generation of pianists was based not on a lack of ability in the realm of performance but on a concern for the transmittal of a great wealth of knowledge to the next wave of pianists and teachers. How fortunate we are for the work in the piano studio done by Josef and Rosina Lhevinne. Russell Sherman, by all accounts a prolific and unique voice on the concert stage and on recordings, had every opportunity to focus all of his artistic efforts on his own craft. His dedication not only to his students but also to teachers and performers around the globe through his book *Piano Pieces*, is indispensable. We owe this luminary a great debt for what was essentially a selfless act in his pursuit of the art of teaching instead of a prominent career as a performing artist.

SOME OF HISTORY'S GREAT PIANO TEACHERS

While studying the lives and careers of the great teachers will give us a toolkit of best practices for working with pupils, if nothing else, it should provide us with great inspiration and a vote of confidence in the important work that we do on a daily basis. Piano teaching will never be an easy job and will likely never be the most lucrative career path, but it is essential, life-changing work that has been handed down by some of the greatest thinkers in Western culture. We deserve a measure of pride, honor, and delight in this profound fact.

NOTES

1. Wendy Powers, "The Piano: The Pianofortes of Bartolomeo Cristofori (1655–1731)," in *Heilbrunn Timeline of Art History* (New York: The Metropolitan Museum of Art, 2000). http://www.metmuseum.org/toah/hd/cris/hd_cris.htm (October 2003).
2. Harold C. Schonberg, *The Great Pianists* (New York: Simon and Schuster, 1987).
3. Wolfgang Amadeus Mozart, Stanley Sadie, and Fiona Smart, *The Letters of Mozart and His Family* (London: Palgrave Macmillan, 1966).
4. Maynard Solomon, "Mozart's Journey to Berlin," *Journal of Musicology* 12, no. 1 (1994): 76–84.
5. Michael Lorenz, "New and Old Documents Concerning Mozart's Pupils Barbara Ployer and Josepha Auernhammer," *Eighteenth-Century Music* 3, no. 2 (2006): 311–322.
6. Erich Hertzmann, "Mozart and Attwood," *Journal of the American Musicological Society* 12, nos. 2–3 (1959): 178–184.
7. Wan-hsuan Wu, *Beethoven through Liszt: Myth, Performance* (PhD diss., The University of Texas at Austin, 2007).
8. Arthur Friedheim, *Life and Liszt: The Recollections of a Concert Pianist* (Mineola: Courier Corporation, 2013).
9. Amy Fay, *Music-Study in Germany: From the Home Correspondence of Amy Fay*, ed. Melusina Fay Peirce (Chicago: A. C. McClurg, 1886).
10. David Lloyd-Jones, "Borodin on Liszt," *Music and Letters* 42, no. 2 (1961): 117–126.

11. Fay, Amy, *Music-Study in Germany: The Classic Memoir of the Romantic Era* (Courier Corporation, 2014): 213.
12. Josef Lhevinne, *Basic Principles in Pianoforte Playing* (Courier Corporation, 2013).
13. Robert K. Wallace, *A Century of Music-Making: The Lives of Josef and Rosina Lhevinne* (Bloomington: Indiana University Press, 1976).
14. Bernard Holland, "Adele Marcus Is Dead at 89; Taught Many Notable Pianists," *New York Times*, May 5, 1995. Accessed February 2, 2017. https://www.nytimes.com/1995/05/05/obituaries/adele-marcus-is-dead-at-89-taught-many-notable-pianists.html.
15. Adele Marcus, Gina Bachauer, Jorge Bolet, Karl Ulrich Schnabel, Claude Frank, Rudolf Firkušný, and Alicia de Larrocha. *Great Pianists Speak with Adele Marcus* (Neptune: Paganiniana Publications, 1979).
16. "Leon Fleisher: 'My life fell apart . . . ;'" *Independent*, May 30, 2010. Accessed January 20, 2017. https://www.independent.co.uk/arts-entertainment/music/features/leon-fleisher-my-life-fell-apart-1984408.html.
17. Frances Stead Sellers, "In a Top-Floor studio, Conductor and Teacher Leon Fleisher Aims for the Musical Heights," *Washington Post*, July 12, 2014. Accessed March 3, 2017. https://www.washingtonpost.com/entertainment/music/in-a-top-floor-studio-conductor-and-teacher-leon-fleisher-aims-for-the-musical-heights/2014/07/10/ea27fe18-fbc8-11e3-8176-f2c941cf35f1_story.html?utm_term=.eeba05a22dba.
18. Sherman, Russell, *Piano pieces* (London: Macmillan, 1997): xi.
19. Jeremy Eichler, "Piano Forte: A Reclusive Keyboard Guru, Boston Artist Peers out at the Universe through 88 keys," *The Boston Globe*, March 21, 2010. Accessed April 4, 2017. http://archive.boston.com/ae/music/articles/2010/03/21/russell_sherman_remains_driven_by_his_art_inspired_by_interpretation/.

Chapter 12

Bringing It All Together

Your Studio as a Diverse Set of Individuals

Piano teaching is a vocational pursuit like no other. Combining the intimacy and personal impact of individual psychology with the skill level of law or medicine practiced at the highest level, our field requires tremendous knowledge, training, practice, empathy, energy, and sensitivity on a daily basis. Coupled with administrative chops and a real business sense, this single job can sometimes feel like four. Yet we persist as teachers because of the nobility and importance of the pursuit. Impacting the lives of young people in a positive way through a sense of achievement, through hard work, and through a rigorous arts education that requires high-level thinking and critical processing is clearly a worthwhile task. The handing down of the great and important art of Western classical music is essential to the survival of our field. The teacher's part in this is indispensable. All of these reasons to do this job are true and important. Nonetheless, what is in it for the teacher, whose daily student-centered approach is selfless and unassuming, whose years of training may approach the level of an M.D., and whose daily dedication to students is often unrecognized? I argue that this profession is so satisfying because of the diversity of our students. Our studios are microcosms of the world around us, with each student affording the teacher an opportunity to rethink his or her pedagogy in its entirety to best meet the needs of that individual. I am daily thankful that there is no homogeneity in my teaching studio. Despite seasons when the cultural or demographic backgrounds of my students may become more similar on a superficial level, each and every student is an individual whom I need to get to know quite deeply in order to assist him or her on the road to becoming the best performer or teacher possible. This is a task that will challenge me throughout my career and a task that invigorates me and makes me want to come to work every day. I would assume that many piano teachers, should they take a moment to examine their motivations for their vocation, would say something similar.

SOCIETAL DIVERSITY IN THE PIANO STUDIO

The United States is an increasingly diverse place. The very concept of our national diversity has become a wedge in today's political landscape. Whatever your personal viewpoint of the strengths or dangers of the unfolding of diversity on a number of fronts in our society, the reality is that America's youth make up an ever-increasingly diverse and differentiated group. Currently, the majority of newborn babies are from racial and ethnic minority populations. United States Census Bureau projections predict that by 2043, non-Hispanic whites will cease to be a majority of the American population.[1] In general, diversity in America is powered by varied fertility rates among racial and ethnic groups, changes in the racial composition of women of ages that might be considered childbearing, and immigration.

About 37 percent of the U.S. population belonged to a racial or ethnic minority in 2012. To put this number into perspective, in

1990, 32 percent of the population under age twenty was from a minority group. This figure increased to 39 percent by the year 2000. By July 2012, 47 percent of the 82.5 million people below the age of twenty in the United States were from minority groups.[2] In contrast to older population groups within the United States, minorities represented only 33 percent of the 231.4 million residents of the United States age twenty or older.[3] In order to further illustrate the point that the youngest members of our society represent the sector where diversity is most rapidly expanding, one can compare preschool-age children with older teenagers. Minorities represented 48 percent of the population under age five in 2012 but only 43 percent of those aged fifteen to nineteen. America is an increasingly diverse place, and, barring any major changes to immigration policy (which seems entirely possible in the post-2016 political climate) or birth rates, this trend will continue at an ever-increasing rate.

The arrival of nearly one million immigrants to the United States annually, mostly from Latin America and Asia, has fanned debate about multiculturalism, social fragmentation, inclusion, and assimilation. Issues of the predominance of English, the abundance of multiracial population centers, and the political and economic power of minority groups will only increase in significance. As is frequently evidenced by the current climate of political rhetoric, important but often alarmist questions about the safety of such an immigration climate and the "Americanness" of our society will continue to be raised, and with much greater frequency. The reality remains, at least for the time being, that racial diversity is increasing and will continue to increase into the foreseeable future. The United States of America is essentially becoming a "majority-minority" society, with children having more impact than any other age group.

The statistics about racial diversity may be dazzling, and sometimes come across as downright confusing, yet the implications for music teachers are vast and far-reaching. Youth in the United States are increasingly diverse, but populations of the elderly continue to be predominantly white. Youth may have power in numbers, but their power in terms of economic and political influence is clearly superseded by that of older individuals. This poses interesting questions and problems for music teachers to consider. Will older and predominantly white American residents vote to raise taxes to assist public schools that teach young people who are quite different from them in ethnical or racial terms? Will this older population support arts education programs for these young people? To look at this dilemma from a bit of a reverse perspective raises even more essential questions for music teachers. Will an increasingly ethnically diverse young population continue to want to study Western classical music, the bedrock of piano teaching since its inception? Piano teachers would be wise to consider the multitude of implications brought about by the changing ethnic demographics of American society. These trends will require us to consider not only the traditional financial support structures of the arts for young people but also the ways in which we hope to reach the youngest students who, at least in the foreseeable future, are going to have quite a different profile from students we have worked with before now.

When we take a step back from these racial statistics, we realize that race and ethnicity form only part of the picture of diversity in the United States. As I have discussed in previous chapters in this volume, students with disabilities and special needs are among the young people we are teaching or may teach in the future. The Individuals with Disabilities Act (IDEA), which was enacted in 1975, mandates that children and youth between the ages of three and twenty-one with disabilities and special needs be provided a free and developmentally appropriate public school education. The percentage of total public school enrollment of children served by federally financed special education programs increased from 83 percent to 13.8 percent between 1976 and 2005.[4] It is difficult to pinpoint whether this increase is a result of increasing numbers of cases of disability, better identification, or better social services, however, it is interesting to note that the percentage of students identified as having specific learning disabilities was 1.8 percent in 1976 and rose to 5.7 percent by 2005.[5] The percentage of students with autism spectrum disorders alone rose from 0.4 percent to 1.1 percent between 1976 and 2005. The numbers don't lie: There are increasing numbers of students with special needs in our public schools and therefore increasing numbers of students with special needs who are at the age when they might be interested in piano study.

Public educators have not shied away from this challenge. Public school systems have a range of specialists who are trained to work with children in need of special education, whether classified as having physical, learning, or emotional issues. Regular classroom teachers are trained to a certain extent to work with students in need of special education and may use tactics within their classroom or in an external setting that are meant to assist a student in need of extra help. Children may also be eligible for what are sometimes called "related services," including counseling, speech therapy, physical therapy, and occupational therapy. In most public schools, if parents believe that their child may have a disability, they have the power based on federal law to ask their school in writing for an evaluation by a psychologist, who will administer a set of tests to determine the kind of extra help that the child may need. These types of evaluations can also be done by a referred specialist in consultation with a child's physician. Although the latter procedure is often expensive, and the cost is borne by the family, the results are honored in public school settings. Once one of these types of evaluations is complete, a public school staff will recommend a document called an IEP (individual education plan). Once this plan is created, a parent must approve it. The IEP is essentially a legal document that describes the services to which a child is entitled through his or her public school, as well as related services.

At times, children with disabilities simply need inexpensive changes in classroom routines that are fairly easy to implement to help them in their schooling. As an example, a child with a learning disability may simply need some extra time when taking tests. Another example would be a child with a significant visual impairment needing books with larger print. These types of changes are called 504 accommodations, after section 504 of the Rehabilitation Act of 1973, which banned discrimination on the basis of physical or mental disability in federally funded programs. Every American public school is required to employ a designated 504 coordinator. When contacted with accommodation requests, the 504 coordinator must schedule a meeting with parents and teachers within thirty days.[6] Like an IEP, a 504 plan is a legal document that the school must follow. Additional resources, which vary slightly from state to state, are available to a student in a public school. Though not perfect, our public schools are generally well equipped to provide services and resources to students with special needs thanks to federal laws, statutes, and mandates.

Obviously, piano teaching does not fall under the purview of such laws, and piano teachers may not be as well trained or equipped to successfully work with students with special needs as are public classroom teachers. Piano teachers would be wise to seek out training and community resources in order to better work with students with special needs for a variety of reasons. First and always foremost, doing so places their education at the forefront of your practice. When you approach your work with a student-centered focus, the students' experience will be richer, more impactful, and more meaningful. Yet expanding your toolbox of teaching techniques also has myriad benefits for your teaching and business life. With the ever-increasing numbers of young people in our society with a variety of special needs, and with those young people often being supported by loving and caring parents who are interested in seeking out the best experiences for their children, an entrepreneurial opportunity exists for a teacher who might decide to become the go-to person in the community for the teaching of special needs. Furthermore, providing a positive experience for a student with special needs is personally enriching. What satisfaction can be gained from bringing positivity, beauty, and light to a young person with special needs, while also possibly improving his or her communicative abilities through the language of music!

DIVERSE PIANO PERSONALITIES

Beyond these more obvious forms of diversity, the personalities of individuals may be the type of diversity most commonly encountered by piano teachers in their daily work. Vast amounts of research have been carried out in the field of psychology about personality types and how these differences manifest themselves in individuals of all ages and developmental stages. Perhaps the most well known, accessible, and useful tool for identifying and understanding personality types is the Myers-Briggs Type Indicator (MBTI), a self-reported questionnaire designed to determine psychological preferences in how individuals perceive the world around them and make decisions in their specific setting. The MBTI, designed by Katharine Cook Briggs and her daughter Isabel Briggs Myers, is based on the typological theory proposed by the noted psychologist Carl Jung, who believed that there are four principal psychological functions within which humans experience the world around them and that one of these four is dominant in an individual most of the time.[7] The MBTI was created in order to more accurately and more specifically measure naturally occurring personality differences in the general population

Jung's theory was founded on his extensive research, which was based mainly on clinical observation. The functions he identified included *thinking, feeling, sensation,* and *intuition*. Each of these cognitive functions had one of two polar orientations: *extraversion* and *introversion*. When combined, a total of eight dominant functions existed in Jung's theory. The MBTI is based on these eight functions, with some minor differences. Jung believed that personality types within his model were similar to the concept of left- or right-handedness in that humans are either born with or develop specific preferred ways of deciding and perceiving. The MBTI sorts these psychological differences into four opposite pairs, referred to by the researchers as "dichotomies," with a total of sixteen possible psychological types. It is important to note that none of these types are meant to be preferable or less-than-preferable; however, Myers and Briggs believed that people instinctually prefer one overall combination of types in their daily lives.

The sixteen personality types included in the MBTI are usually referred to by four letters that are the initial letters of each of their four type preferences (in the case of *intuition*, an *N* is used in order to distinguish it from *introversion*). Examples of personality type abbreviations in the MBTI include ENTP (extroversion, intuition, thinking, perception) or INFP (introversion, intuition, feeling, perception). The MBTI states that the person taking the test is always the best judge of his or her preferences.

The MBTI consists of ninety-three "forced-choice" questions, which means there are only two possible answers to each question. Participants are allowed to skip questions if they feel they are unable to choose between the two possible answers. After taking the test, participants are provided their score, which includes a bar graph and an indication of how many points they received in certain categories. In the MBTI, the terms *introvert* and *extravert* are referred to as attitudes. An introvert is typically more interested in the inner world of ideas, and an extravert prefers the outer world of people and things around them. *Sensing* and *intuition* are the perceiving functions in the MBTI. Jung referred to these functions as the "irrational functions." He intended this label as a technical term and not as a negative term. Jung believed that a person does not have control over receiving information but only how to process it once received.[8] Sensing people tend to focus on the present and on concrete information gained from the world around them by their senses. Intuitive people tend to focus on the future and tend to pick up on patterns and possibilities more easily. One might describe an intuitive person as someone who receives information from his or her subconscious or someone who perceives relationships by way of insights.

Thinking and *Feeling* are the decision-making aspects of the MBTI. Both thinking and feeling individuals attempt to make logical choices in their lives, with thinking people tending to make decisions based on logical connections and feeling people making decisions based on a value system they have developed or on concerns about how a decision may impact people around them. To put this in the simplest of terms, thinking individuals decide with their brains, while feeling individuals decide with their hearts. This particular category of classifications within the MBTI has particular resonance regarding students of music: Consider the ways in which your students approach performances, some with particular strengths in analysis and control and some with particular strengths in passion and emotion.

Judging and *perceiving* refer to the sensing/intuition and thinking/feeling dichotomies described above. *Judging and perceiving* indicate which of the two dichotomies is utilized by individuals when dealing with the world around them. Judging types tend to like a planned, organized and logical approach to life. Perceiving types prefer a flexible and spontaneous approach to most tasks, wanting to keep any and all possibilities open. Again, the implications for teachers of piano are immense when considering these two dichotomies. Might perceiving individuals be more open to improvisation than judging individuals? Might judging students approach the study of tonal harmony with a more step-by-step approach than perceiving ones? Might perceiving individuals be more amenable to learning by rote than judging individuals? Generally, the latter prefer a planned, "left brain" approach to life and thrive on rules and procedures that are clear and even externally applied. On the opposite end of the spectrum, perceiving types prefer a spontaneous daily approach and rely on on-the-spot judgments.

When two, three, or four preferences are known within the framework of the MBTI, a type dynamic beings to emerge. When a total of four preferences are combined, it is called an MBTI type. In total there are sixteen unique types and many more possible two- and three-letter combinations, each with a descriptive name.

The test has received a fair amount of criticism regarding its scientific accuracy because the bulk of the data collected come from anecdote and introspection. In addition, the scientific reliability of this examination is considered low because those who retake the test frequently are assigned a different MBTI type.[9] The test has somewhat frequently been used in career-planning settings, moreover, without significant studies of how well any resulting career-planning advice plays out. I would not suggest that piano teachers administer Myer-Briggs Type Indicator examinations to each of their students and plan curriculum and lessons on the results. Reducing such a nuanced and subtle pursuit as teaching in the arts to a somewhat dry and scientific analysis would almost certainly be an exercise in disappointment. Nonetheless, studying the diversity among the sixteen types possible in the MBTI poses the astonishing challenge of assessing the tremendous possible diversity of personality types in a piano studio. An ESFP (extraverted, sensing, feeling, perceiving) individual may be a natural performer who has a need to connect with others. An ESFP may be a lively and attractive personality on stage who loves to be the center of attention. Yet such a student may become overwhelmed by too much criticism and by negative thoughts. As a sort of opposite of the ESFP, the INTJ (introverted, intuitive, extraverted, thinking) type focuses a large part of life internally, taking in stimuli from the world in the form of intuition. The INTJ plans and strategizes and values competence, knowledge, and the improvement of intelligence. This type observes what is going on around him or her and create possibilities based on these observations "scientifically." Primarily, an INTJ values organization and systems for learning. What might an ESFP's strength be when it comes to the study of music? One might expect such a pupil to be an exceptional performer, confident and excited about the prospect of sharing his or her music on the stage, even in the most strenuous circumstances. However, the same student may be particularly wounded by harsh criticism from a competition judge. An INTJ may not have the same willingness to relish the spotlight of performance but may be apt to provide excellent and probing analysis of the works he or she is studying, providing another level of nuance and strength to performances learned systematically and carefully.

In my interactions with excellent teachers, I have come to realize that these teachers, though they may not be very familiar with the MBTI, somehow are able to make at least an informal inventory of their students' personality types. Such sensitive and intuitive teachers are capable of quickly sensing their students' profile in their weekly interactions, tailoring the curriculum to their students' needs, while highlighting their strengths in a way that builds up their sense of self-worth and self-efficacy. A willingness to explore a personality inventory like the MBTI may be a stepping stone to developing this sort of intuition in one's teaching.

WRITING EXPERCISE: Take an online Myer-Briggs Type Indicator such as the one found at https://www.16personalities.com. Discuss the results of your test with your classmates. Write about how your piano teaching might be affected by knowing the MBTI types of your students.

Howard Gardner's theory of multiple intelligences is another way of thinking about the diversity of human thinking. In his 1983 book *Frames of Mind: The Theory of Multiple Intelligences*, Gardner states that an intelligence must meet eight separate criteria:

1. The potential for brain isolation by brain damage
2. The place in evolutionary history
3. The presence of core operations
4. The susceptibility to encoding, or symbolic expression
5. A distinct developmental progression
6. The existence of savants, prodigies and other exceptional people
7. The support from experimental psychology
8. The support from psychometric findings.[10]

Gardner, with Thomas Hatch, described eight abilities that he believed could assist in meeting these criteria:

1. Musical-rhythmic: Particular sensitivity to sounds, rhythms, tones and music. Individuals with high musical intelligence may have a well-developed sense of pitch or perfect pitch, and are able to sing, play musical instruments, or compose.
2. Visual-spatial: The ability to visualize with an inner-eye, and judge spatial relationships.
3. Verbal-linguistic: An excellent ability with words and languages. These individuals are typically good at reading, writing, telling stories and memorizing words and dates.
4. Logical-mathematical: An intelligence that has to do with logic, reasoning, numbers and critical thinking.
5. Bodily-kinesthetic: The control of one's body and the capacity to handle objects skillfully. Also sometimes an advanced sense of timing and the ability to train responses. Gardner believes that careers that suit this group of learners may include [those of] athletes, dancers, musicians, actors, builders, police officers and soldiers.
6. Interpersonal: Individuals who are skillful in their sensitivity to others' moods, feelings, temperaments, motivations, and their ability to cooperate in order to work as part of a group.
7. Intrapersonal: Individuals with a deep understanding of the self with typically advanced introspective and self-reflective capacities.
8. Naturalistic: An individual who is able to easily make distinctions in the natural world, and to use this ability productively. These individuals may have an enhanced concept of the role of humanity within the greater natural world.[11]

Although Gardner describes the differences between these intelligences in much detail, he opposed the idea of labeling learners using one of these intelligences. According to the author, an intelligence is "a biopsychological potential to process information that can be activated in a cultural setting to solve problems or create products that are of value in a culture."[12] Gardner believed that the purpose of schooling should be to develop intelligences and to help people reach vocational goals that are appropriate to their particular spectrum of intelligences.

There has been much criticism of Gardner's theory of multiple intelligences, much of which is based on the fact that very little of this theory has been tested empirically. Nonetheless, the breakdown of intellectual strengths may have resonance for the seasoned music educator who has likely encountered students from each of these groups. Perhaps one of the strengths of piano study is that it lies at the crossroads of so many of these categories. There is no denying that developing a student's musical-rhythmic and harmonic intelligence is a goal of the piano teacher, but a highly developed and well-trained pianist will also have advanced abilities in each of the other categories as laid out by Gardner. For example, the visual-spatial intelligence may lead to security in memorization, whereas bodily-kinesthetic training and development are necessary in order for a pianist to play increasingly complex textures. The naturalistic intelligence may find a connection with pieces about the natural world, of which there are many in the canon of piano repertoire, while the verbal-linguistic individual will find an easy and natural ability in addressing his or her audience and may some day prove to be an excellent piano teacher.

Additional models of learning styles include the Keirsey Temperament Sorter (KTS), which is a self-assessed personality questionnaire closely associated with the MBTI (described above), and the VAK/VARK model (Visual Learning, Auditory Learning, Read/Write Learning, Kinesthetic Learning). The KTS is a particularly popular model for assessment of employees in the business world, and the VARK may prove to be a model that piano teachers would find useful for understanding how their students experience learning. Piano teachers would be well advised to explore a number of these learning theories, because the diversity of learners may prove to be one of the most fascinating and important aspects of delivering effective instruction.

THE DIVERSITY OF HUMAN DEVELOPMENT

Beyond the diversity of ethnicity, special needs, and personality types, the diversity of developmental needs and abilities based on age among our students is significant. The life of a child is a time of rapid growth and development, with different needs and stressors affecting different age groups. Needs continue to change beyond the age of eighteen, as outlined in chapters on teaching undergraduate and graduate students in this book. Furthermore, adults, during different seasons of their lives, have different strengths and challenges based on issues such as brain plasticity and stresses brought about by jobs, family responsibilities, retirement, or any number of things.

Average emotional-developmental milestones based on age are well understood by piano teachers who have pupils with a wide range of ages. Within the field of psychology, the term *early childhood* is usually defined as the time period from the age of two until the age of six or seven years.[13] During early childhood, there is significant synaptic growth of neural fibers in the brain. At this time the brain increases from 70 percent of its potential adult weight to 90 percent.[14] This tremendous physical growth of the brain is coupled with a major increase in cognitive abilities. By about the age of five, children are typically able to speak in advanced ways and have usually mastered most basic aspects of eye-hand coordination.[15] In children, large muscles (involving gross motor skills) develop before small muscles (for fine motor skills) do. This is clearly applicable topic to piano teaching. Use of the fingers on the keyboard would involve advanced skill for a person in early childhood. Teachers would be wise to focus first on the larger motor skills of piano playing, including the use of the torso, the use of the upper arms, and the use of the entire hand rather than the early use of the individual fingers.

Early childhood is the stage during which children repeatedly ask questions, most notably "why?" Children at this stage are not yet able to use abstract thought. They think literally. For example, a child who is told, "Give me a minute," may imagine someone handing over a physical piece of time. Or, a child who hits his or her head on a table may label the table "bad." These types of identifications are typical of children of this age. Piano teachers should consider this stage of cognitive development when teaching young students. A student who makes a mistake in a recital may label the piece bad. Children at this age are typically not yet able to positively attribute mistakes to causes under their control.

Young students, especially those who are preadolescent, may be fearless about performing. How many young pianists have you witnessed who simply do not get nervous when faced with a performing situation? Why is this? Is it that students before the age of adolescence have yet to value the opinions of peers? I'm not sure that the answer is so clear-cut, but there is likely some truth to this theory. Many young pianists value achievement, but that achievement is typically based on extrinsic motivators. Trophies and certificates, as well as class recitals that feature sweet baked treats afterward, are enough to instill a sense of focus, drive, and purpose in many young students. Before the age of ten or eleven, perhaps, students may be primarily concerned with the safety and security of their family situation, the authority of their parents and teachers, and the fellowship of a close group of friends. This is not to say that young students are somehow superhuman in their ability to learn quickly and to perform without a hint of insecurity. Surely, the lives children are full of drama and tumult as they learn about emotions and how to appropriately manage them. My heart sinks every time my six-year-old daughter has a temper tantrum and then apologizes because she couldn't control it. That being said, preadolescence is a time of discovery, a time of nearly limitless learning and acquisition, and a period of a certain amount of fearlessness and refreshing lack of self-awareness.

The adolescent child is generally in a time of great change and tumult, physically, emotionally, socially, and even neurologically. Adolescence is essentially a transitional stage of physical and psychological development that generally occurs during the period from puberty to legal adulthood, which is not the exact same age for every person.[16] Although adolescence is sometimes considered to coincide with the teenage years, its physical, psychological, and cultural markers may begin much earlier and end much later than the end of the teenage years. In most young people puberty now begins during the period before adolescence (sometimes referred to as preadolescence), and physical and cognitive growth traditionally associated with adolescence can extend well into the early twenties. Age only provides a general marker of adolescence. Understanding the adolescent human being requires information gleaned from many different fields, including anthropology, sociology, education, history, biology, and psychology. Adolescence is perhaps the most volatile period of growth and change in the life of a human being. Multiple transitions are taking place during this time, including the move from primary to secondary school, an eventual transition to employment, and changes in living circumstances, including concepts of increased independence and responsibility in most parts of one's life. Defined in biological terms, adolescence is marked by the physical transitional period from the onset of puberty to the termination of physical growth, and in cognitive terms it involves changes in the ability to think in the abstract and in multiple dimensions.[17] However, different cultural and familial contexts do not paint such a clear picture about the beginning and end of this critical and challenging period in early life.

Perhaps most important for the piano teacher, adolescence is a time when critical changes occur in the human brain, which is not fully developed by the time a person reaches puberty. Between the ages of ten and twenty-five the human brain undergoes massive changes that have particularly important implications for behavioral functions. The brain usually reaches 90 percent of its adult size by the time a human reaches the age of six.[18] As a result of this early growth, the brain does not expand much in size during adolescence. It does, however, expand physically in the complexity of its folds, particularly in the parts of the cortex that process cognitive and emotional behavior.[19] Through a process called synaptic pruning, unnecessary neuronal connections in the brain are eliminated during adolescence. This does not mean that the brain loses skills and functionality; rather, it becomes more efficient owing to the reduction of unused pathways.[20] The first areas of the human brain to be pruned are those involving primary functions, which are mostly motor and sensory areas.[21] Some of the largest changes in the brain during adolescence happen in the prefrontal cortex, which is involved in cognitive control and decision making. During adolescence, synaptic pruning in the prefrontal cortex increases, typically improving the efficiency of information processing as well as neural connections between the prefrontal cortex and other regions of the brain, which are strengthened as a result of this pruning. Essentially, the adolescent brain is better able to evaluate risks and rewards and has improved control over impulsivity. When someone who works with children considers the differences in behavior between the child and the adolescent, this latter point makes particular sense.[22]

Adolescence is also a time during which massive cognitive development occurs. Adolescence can be described as the time in the human life cycle during which an individual's thoughts explore the abstract for the first time. Because of this development, the adolescent human may be able to think and reason more widely, applying concepts learned in smaller, non-applied forms to the world around him or her.

By the time most individuals have reached the age of fifteen, their cognitive abilities are essentially comparable to those of an adult. During this period of life, cognitive ability improves mainly in the following categories:

1. Organization: Adolescents are typically more aware of their thought process, and the organization of information.
2. Speed of processing: Adolescents think at a quicker speed than children.
3. Memory: Short-term ("working memory") and long-term memory improve in the adolescent brain.
4. Attention: "Selective attention," the process of focusing on one bit of stimulus while tuning out another, and "divided attention," the skill of paying attention to two or more stimuli at the same time, improves in the adolescent brain.[23]

Adolescents also gain the ability to engage in the skill of "metacognition," that is, thinking about thinking itself. This increase in their knowledge base as it relates to their personal patterns of thinking leads to advantages such as more effective and independent studying.

Metacognition is also related to the concepts of increased introspection and self-consciousness.[24] How often have students who have studied piano from the time they were young children suddenly developed stage fright and nervousness when they approached adolescence? Perhaps these very typical struggles are not related to practicing and training at all but, rather, to the changing brain.

It may seem strange to speak about the concept of wisdom when it comes to the adolescent student, but the development of wisdom, which could be defined as the ability to use insight and judgment developed through experience, is another hallmark of the changes in the adolescent brain. Wisdom and intelligence are not the same thing. Adolescents typically do not improve substantially on IQ tests taken in childhood.[25]

Perhaps even more important than the biological changes that occur in the brain of the adolescent are the social changes that occur through the concept of identity development, which is perhaps the aspect of change that is the most crucial when students are pursuing the study of the piano. For most individuals in most societies, the search for identity begins in adolescence.[26] Attempting to find their own identity and discover who they are, adolescents typically try on a number of different identities in the search for the one that represents them the most. Developing an identity at this time is a monumental task because of a number of social pressures that weigh particularly heavily on the life of an adolescent. Identity is impacted by family life and expectations, the general social environment, and social status. Researchers typically use three general approaches to understanding the development of identity: self-esteem, sense of identity, and self-concept.[27] These approaches have a tremendous impact on an emerging pianist. Self-esteem, vitally important to the concept of identity development, may drive young musicians toward identifying as serious musicians or away from this identity. Clearly, providing positive performance and competition experiences can make or break young pianists who may be making decisions on some level about how closely they identify with their musical study. Self-concept could be defined as the ability of a person to have beliefs about the self that are clearly defined, consistent, and firmly established. Within the realm of self-concept, adolescents learn to imagine multiple "possible individuals" that they could become as a result of their choices. Perhaps most important, self-concept involves the idea of "differentiation," that is, how a person's behavior influences his or her perception of others.[28] A piano teacher would be wise to develop partnerships within the studio, with frameworks that are positive and uplifting. Given the importance of students' perception of the other during this stage, monitoring friendly rivalries in a studio, while being careful not to create situations when unnecessary competition and jealousies occur, would be beneficial to students in this stage of development.

Sense of identity centers on the idea of egocentrism in that adolescents feels a self-conscious desire to feel accepted and important in their peer groups.[29] During this period individuals care deeply about their membership in crowds perceived as desirable. Being "cool," as determined by influential members of an individual's social circles, becomes paramount. Adolescents may attempt to define themselves based on fashion and other superficial constructs, as well as altering their media and entertainment consumption based on social desirability. This point is critical for teachers of piano. I would guess that classical music is not the preferred genre in the social circles of most American youth. Students of piano may feel a sense of dissonance between what they are studying and what is considered cool. Teachers should try to face this reality head-on. Framing classical music as an exciting and worthwhile pursuit can go a long way in developing a sense of identity in an adolescent.

Furthermore, creating opportunities for engagement with classical music for adolescent students and their peers can break down the walls between consumption of socially fashionable media and great art music. The teacher of adolescents may consider developing outreach programs for the friends of their students, inviting them to performances by the local symphony orchestra or to chamber music concerts by faculty at the local university. A sort of classical proselytizing may help normalize the consumption of classical music within a student's peer group and might even make it hip when presented with excitement and genuine enthusiasm.

WRITING EXERCISE: Develop a plan for activities that would provide exposure to classical music for teens in your studio that would include their friends. Include possible debriefing exercises that would help extend the impact of this kind of exposure in students to whom classical music might be new.

As is obvious from the enormous biological, psychological, and social complexities in the life of an adolescent, this stage is critical and unique within the scope of overall human development. This is also the age at which many students of piano cease their studies. This is not surprising, considering the tremendous tumult that is going on in the brain alone. The teacher of the adolescent would be wise to seek out as much current research as possible about this age range and attempt to develop and adjust curricula and teaching strategies for the specific stressors involved.

Diversity in our teaching studios is simply a result of the diversity of the culture that surrounds us. It would be incorrect, even in a superficially homogeneous teaching studio, to assume that our students come from the same or similar backgrounds. Contemplating and understanding the differences that surround us can create inspiring new challenges in our teaching. In addition, understanding the specific needs of each of our students based on their uniqueness in any number of ways can help us better serve our students. Difference and diversity are qualities to be embraced. The opportunity to work with individuals one-on-one brings these unique qualities to the forefront of the teaching and mentoring relationship. This is a quality in teaching to be celebrated!

NOTES

1. United States Census Bureau, *U.S. Census Bureau Projections Show a Slower Growing, Older, More Diverse Nation a Half Century from Now*, 2012. Accessed July 8, 2018. https://www.census.gov/newsroom/releases/archives/population/cb12-243.html.
2. Kenneth M. Johnson, Andrew Schaefer, Daniel T. Lichter, and Luke T. Rogers, "The Increasing Diversity of America's Youth," *The Carsey School of Public Policy at the Scholars' Repository* (2014): 212.
3. Grayson K. Vincent and Victoria Averil Velkoff, *The Next Four Decades: The Older Population in the United States, 2010 to 2050*. No. 1138 (Washington, D.C.: U.S. Department of Commerce, Economics and Statistics Administration, U.S. Census Bureau, 2010): 5.
4. Candace Cortiella and Sheldon H. Horowitz, *The State of Learning Disabilities: Facts, Trends and Emerging Issues* (New York: National Center for Learning Disabilities, 2014).
5. Ibid.
6. H. Rutherford Turnbull, Nancy Huerta, Matt Stowe, Louis Weldon, and Suzanne Schrandt, *The Individuals with Disabilities Education Act as Amended in 2004* (Boston: Pearson, 2009).
7. Douglas A. MacDonald, Peter E. Anderson, Catherine I. Tsagarakis, and Cornelius J. Holland, "Examination of the Relationship between the Myers-Briggs Type Indicator and the NEO Personality Inventory," *Psychological Reports* 74, no. 1 (1994): 339–344.
8. Isabel Briggs Meyers, Mary H. McCaulley, and Allen L. Hammer, *Introduction to Type: A Description of the Theory and Applications of the Myers-Briggs Type Indicator* (Consulting Psychologists Press, 1990).
9. Richard N. Landers, Paul R. Sackett, and Kathy A. Tuzinski, "Retesting after Initial Failure, Coaching Rumors, and Warnings against Faking in Online Personality Measures for Selection," *Journal of Applied Psychology* 96, no. 1 (2011): 202.

10. Jonathan Plucker and Amber Esping, eds., *Human Intelligence: Historical Influences, Current Controversies, Teaching Resources*, 2014. Accessed July 8, 2018. http://www.intelltheory.com.
11. Howard Gardner and Thomas Hatch, "Educational Implications of the Theory of Multiple Intelligences," *Educational Researcher* 18, no. 8 (1989): 4.
12. Howard Gardner, *Intelligence Reframed: Multiple Intelligences for the 21st Century* (New York: Basic Books, 2000), 33–34.
13. Robert V. Kail, *Children and Their development* (London: Pearson Education, 2012).
14. Rhoshel K. Lenroot and Jay N. Giedd, "Brain Development in Children and Adolescents: Insights from Anatomical Magnetic Resonance Imaging," *Neuroscience and Biobehavioral Reviews* 30, no. 6 (2006): 719–720.
15. Leo B. Hendry and Marion Kloep, *Lifespan Development: Resources, Challenges and Risks* (Boston: Cengage Learning EMEA, 2002).
16. Cheryl L. Sisk and Douglas L. Foster, "The Neural Basis of Puberty and Adolescence," *Nature Neuroscience* 7, no. 10 (2004): 1040–1047.
17. Sharon E. Paulson and Cheryl L. Sputa, "Patterns of Parenting During Adolescence: Perceptions of Adolescents and Parents," *Adolescence* 31, no. 122 (1996): 369–382.
18. Joan Stiles and Terry L. Jernigan, "The Basics of Brain Development," *Neuropsychology Review* 20, no. 4 (2010): 328.
19. Deborah Yurgelun-Todd, "Emotional and Cognitive Changes During Adolescence," *Current Opinion in Neurobiology* 17, no. 2 (2007): 251–257.
20. Deanna Kuhn, "Do Cognitive Changes Accompany Developments in the Adolescent Brain?" *Perspectives on Psychological Science* 1, no. 1 (2006): 59–67.
21. Sarah-Jayne Blakemore and Suparna Choudhury, "Development of the Adolescent Brain: Implications for Executive Function and Social Cognition," *Journal of Child Psychology and Psychiatry* 47, nos. 3–4 (2006): 296–312.
22. Linda P. Spear, "The Adolescent Brain and Age-Related Behavioral Manifestations," *Neuroscience and Biobehavioral Reviews* 24, no. 4 (2000): 417–463.
23. Adele Diamond, "Attention-Deficit Disorder (Attention-Deficit/Hyperactivity Disorder without Hyperactivity): A Neurobiologically and Behaviorally Distinct Disorder from Attention-Deficit/Hyperactivity Disorder (with Hyperactivity)," *Development and Psychopathology* 17, no. 3 (2005): 817.
24. Scott R. Bishop, Mark Lau, Shauna Shapiro, Linda Carlson, Nicole D. Anderson, James Carmody, Zindel V. Segal, et al., "Mindfulness: A Proposed Operational Definition," *Clinical Psychology: Science and Practice* 11, no. 3 (2004): 230–241.
25. W. Steven Barnett, "Long-Term Effects of Early Childhood Programs on Cognitive and School Outcomes," *Future of Children* (1995): 25–50.

26. Cindy Y. Huang and Elizabeth A. Stormshak, "A Longitudinal Examination of Early Adolescence Ethnic Identity Trajectories," *Cultural Diversity and Ethnic Minority Psychology* 17, no. 3 (2011): 261.
27. Marilynn B. Brewer and Wendi Gardner, "Who Is This 'We'? Levels of Collective Identity and Self-Representations," *Journal of Personality and Social Psychology* 71, no. 1 (1996): 83–93.
28. Maja Deković and Wim Meeus, "Peer Relations in Adolescence: Effects of Parenting and Adolescents' Self-Concept," *Journal of Adolescence* 20, no. 2 (1997): 163–176.
29. Mark Tarrant, "Adolescent Peer Groups and Social Identity," *Social Development* 11, no. 1 (2002): 110–123.

Chapter 13

The Motivated and Inspired Piano Teacher

Piano teaching is a tremendously challenging profession. Requiring rigorous training, typically from a very young age, and sometimes many years of schooling across multiple degree programs, it is a job that typically does not rank highly in terms of pay. Its dividends are in reaching students, making glorious music, and the satisfaction of doing good work. One could argue that classical music is valued less each year in our society, so our vocation is often misunderstood by the public. Sometimes viewed as a quaint throwback reserved for the kindly neighborhood grandmother, piano teaching has a general reputation that might need repairing. All of this, combined with the effort and energy required in the teaching of children, can result in burnout, a lack of focus, and a general malaise about what might have once been a true passion. Piano teachers need to be aware of these dangers, which can easily suck the life out of a career. Wise instructors will proactively find ways to combat these forces with continuing education, innovation in their teaching, a consistent thirst for new knowledge and skills in both teaching and performing, and an attitude that is forgiving of their failings and positive about their opportunities.

PIANO TEACHER TRAINING

Rigorous training in piano performance, literature, piano pedagogy is indispensable for the successful piano teacher. An unfortunate reality of our field is that it is highly unregulated, and it is quite true that anyone who advertises himself as a piano teacher will be able to attract students. Teachers need not be highly qualified or trained in order to make a living in this field. The serious piano teacher will attempt to combat this trend by simply being the finest piano teacher that he or she can be. The amount of initial training required of someone hoping to become an impactful piano teacher who is also a successful businessperson likely rivals the training and schooling required of a doctor or a lawyer. Law school is typically a three-year course beyond the undergraduate degree. Medical school is typically four or five years beyond the undergraduate degree. A prospective piano teacher pursuing an advanced degree in piano pedagogy undergoes at least two years of study for a master's degree and up to six additional years for a doctorate. I'm unsure what the similarities between these training regimens are; however, the implication for piano teachers might be that we need to take our profession quite seriously. Piano teaching should be no less essential in our society than dental care. It's about time we starting acting this way!

Fundamental training in all aspects related to performance and teaching is essential for the qualified piano teacher. High-level training in performance is necessary, with all requisite aspects of technique covered, as well as the obtaining of a comprehensive repertoire of canonical works within the classical tradition. The reasons for this are quite simple and straightforward: The effective teacher will demonstrate at the piano for students. Students of all levels are savvy and have ears that are naturally attuned to quality performance. Furthermore, there is power in teaching by rote, whether it is "Mary Had a Little Lamb" or the Beethoven Sonata op. 109. An ability to demonstrate complete works, as well as smaller passages within works at all levels is an essential quality of the competent teacher.

Pianists are blessed with a repertoire of almost incomprehensible breadth. The number and quality of solo works written for our instrument is unrivaled by those of any other instrument. The thirty-two sonatas of Beethoven make up a fraction of his overall output, yet undertaking the learning and performance of all of these iconic pieces is something that relatively few pianists have attempted. These works while monumental in their technical and musical scope, merely scratch the surface of the repertoire that we have available to us. How does the piano teacher obtain a working knowledge of both the advanced repertoire and the teaching repertoire at beginning and intermediate levels? Many fine piano pedagogy curricula will introduce teachers to works by the great composers from all time periods at all levels. In addition, piano literature courses should be required offerings for teachers of this king of instruments. Knowing opus numbers, keys, and dates of birth might seem like tedium, but obtaining this information is akin to understanding anatomy as a medical doctor. Diagnosis is impossible when the skeletal structure is foreign.

Other subjects that may supplement the knowledge and skills of a piano teacher include psychology, music business and entrepreneurship, chamber music, music in early childhood, musicology, music theory, and piano ensemble repertoire (this list is truly endless). Applying the liberal arts model to a music performance and music-teaching curriculum, and drawing deeply and broadly from this list of subjects, will only make the piano teacher more effective, more passionate, more well-read, more well-informed, more versatile, and more eager (again, this list is truly endless).

WRITING EXERCISE: Reflect on the aspects of your piano and piano pedagogy training that might prove to be strengths as a teacher. Also, reflect on the aspects of your training that might prove to be weaknesses. What steps can you take to improve on these potential weaknesses?

CONTINUING EDUCATION FOR PIANO TEACHERS

Continuing education is an essential element of any field. The average teaching day may be exhausting and quite long. It is difficult to carve time out of such a schedule to practice, to study new teaching repertoire, or to network with colleagues, but teachers who are interested in keeping their skills current and sharp will find a way to do so. I have been greatly encouraged by the number of teachers I have worked with who have been truly eager to take lessons. At the Michigan State University College of Music, we offer a Piano Retreat every other summer, where piano teachers are invited to East Lansing to take lessons with members of the piano faculty over a number of days and to attend workshops. Every teacher who has taken this opportunity has been grateful for it and excited about this time that is dedicated to honing his or her craft. Moreover, some of my hardest-working students have been piano teachers. I teach lessons to a number of piano teachers, some who come very regularly, and some who come only periodically. Effective piano teachers are consistently practicing and consistently seeking feedback on their performance skills. Consider seeking out a master teacher in your area to keep yourself working and to keep yourself accountable to your own ideal performance level.

Regular practicing is essential to the pianist and piano teacher for a number of reasons. Pianists have occasionally been referred to as the Olympic athletes of the small muscles. The technical aspects of playing the piano require a tremendous amount of training and maintenance. While in most pianists the majority of this physical building happens at a young age, muscle atrophy is no less real in the pianist than in the weight lifter. A consistent connection to the instrument and a regular practice routine may keep this atrophy at bay. Furthermore, the act of playing the piano is an advanced neurological activity using brain centers that control complex fine muscle groups as well as using logic and following the theoretical construction of great works. Regular piano practice, thus, is calisthenics for the mind. Consider carving out a small amount of time from your daily schedule to practice finger exercises, scales, and arpeggios as well as old repertoire and new repertoire in order to keep your physical skills fresh and lively. Don't be ashamed that your daily schedule prohibits you from attaining your once-ideal practice time of three to five hours; strive for even thirty minutes to one hour, but be sure to do this every day, and at least most days of the week.

All excellent piano teachers were serious piano students and pianists first. Our identity as pianists grounds us to our early training, to the initial excitement we had for the instrument, and to our time as students who were at one time eager, scared, and enraptured by the excitement and sometimes the mystery of classical piano music. If we abandon the art of creation and practice at the piano, we not only disconnect ourselves from our original experience with the art but also disconnect ourselves from the process of struggle, practice, memorization, and performance creation that our students are going through. Losing this connection to our students' processes creates a rift between them and us, stilting our empathy for their musical journey while not taking seriously the art of quality demonstration in a piano lesson. A quality teacher is not a former pianist, and a pianist is not a future teacher. Our identity, by the very nature of performance, which makes the study of piano unique, is infinitely tied up in the concept of performance being our vocation. Don't allow your connection to your life as a performer to be severed. Both you and your students will be the beneficiaries!

The piano repertoire is immense. If one considers all of the works by just one representative composer from each period, the total number would be more than would be possible to learn in a lifetime. For example, it would be a nearly insurmountable task to learn the complete works of J. S. Bach, the complete works of Ludwig van Beethoven, the complete works of Johannes Brahms, the complete works of Claude Debussy, and the complete works of Sergei Prokofiev (but what a project!). At the advanced level alone, we are blessed with a repertoire that is not approached by that of another instrument. And this number expands when the teaching repertoire is considered. At levels 1–10 of the Royal Conservatory Official Examination Syllabus, 2015 edition (Canada), for example, there are between sixty and one hundred pieces listed *per level*. A well-trained piano pedagogue will not merely be satisfied that these pieces exist, knowing that they can be used in the appropriate circumstance, but will be eager to learn to perform the works with style, command, and aplomb, increasing his or her intimate knowledge of the challenges and teaching advantages of these works. It is just as useful to the teacher to learn to perform any of the op. 10 or op. 25 études of Chopin from level 10 as it is to learn any of the *24 Pieces for Children* of Kabalevsky from level 1. Music from any portion of the piano repertoire, when written by sensitive and pedagogically sound composers, is stimulating and worth learning. In your practice as a pianist, take the time to expand your repertoire as much as possible. Not only will your teaching toolkit of pieces expand, but your musicianship will be sharpened at multiple levels of difficulty and in multiple styles of composition.

To put it very simply, but, I think, very truthfully, piano performance is fun. Taking the time to practice each and every day should be a joyful experience. To the portion of the population outside the business of music, taking up the piano might seem like a truly joyful pursuit and a hobby of great challenge and great relaxation. If piano teachers who are struggling to practice their own instrument took this outsider's view, their perspective on this task might be more positive and conducive to good work. Furthermore, piano teachers should stand as paragons of the beauty and importance of classical music performance in their communities. In order to bring this joy into the society that surrounds you, consider forming a piano practice accountability club with piano teachers in your area. Such a group could produce concerts of great impact and great beauty at places that are hungry for great classical music, for example, retirement homes, hospitals, elementary schools, and prisons.

WRITING EXERCISE: Develop a practicing plan for your life as a piano teacher. How, specifically, will you schedule practicing into your daily schedule? What short-term and long-term goals will you set for yourself to help keep yourself accountable?

Conferences and Workshops

There are more formal continuing education opportunities for teachers that fall into a number of different categories. From summer workshops to national conferences, these offerings vary in price, scope, size, organizational affiliation, and geographical location. A partial listing is given below.

National Conference on Keyboard Pedagogy, for teachers, Lombard, IL, July of every other year.

The National Conference on Keyboard Pedagogy (NCKP) is a biennial meeting of keyboard music educators, researchers, and industry leaders representing all fifty states and over a dozen other nations. Celebrating over 30 years of excellence and innovation in music education at the keyboard, the mission of NCKP is to enhance the quality of music-making throughout life and to educate teachers who are dedicated to nurturing lifelong involvement in music-making from the earliest to the most advanced levels. NCKP offers participants four inspiring, innovative, and challenging days every other summer at the Westin Lombard Yorktown Center in Lombard, IL. http://keyboardpedagogy.org/national-conference-info2

Celebrating The Spectrum: A Festival of Music and Life, ages 12–22, East Lansing, MI, July 16–23, 2017, $1,000 for students (Full tuition scholarships available). Teacher track available.

Celebrating The Spectrum is designed to give qualified advanced pre-College piano students on the Autism Spectrum a preview of a life in music. The daily schedule will reflect the life of a music major in a university setting culminating in two live performances. The first, a "house concert", gives the students an intimate setting to try out their performances prior to the Grand Finale Concert in Cook Recital Hall. All students perform in master classes by College of Music piano faculty Professor Deborah Moriarty and Dr. Derek Kealii Polischuk. The classes will be devoted to solo repertoire and piano four hand repertoire with faculty and student interns. Lectures from Dr. Lauren Harris, Dr. Michael Thaut, and Dr. Scott Price are designed to give participants a feel for the academic class component of a college education. A daily Pilates class introduces students to a "body awareness" approach to playing the piano. http://www.music.msu.edu/spectrum

Taubman Piano Festival, Age 9-Senior, Montclair, New Jersey, Every June.

Dorothy Taubman's Approach to the piano presents principles of coordinated motion that unburden the hands and unleash the spirit. Daily Lectures, Master Classes, mini-group Clinics, Pedagogy Workshops and Evening Recitals.

https://sites.google.com/site/Taubmanfestival2017

Rami's Rhapsody Piano Camp for Adults, Utica NY June and October of every year. $700.

Take a week off just to practice, learn, and perform with like-minded music lovers. Join Rami Bar-Niv, international concert pianist, for a unique opportunity to spend a week in the country, surrounded by a special group of people who share the joys and challenges of being adult piano students, as well as gaining an up close and personal experience with a world class pianist. This camp is suitable for adult piano players of all levels, from complete beginners to professional performers and piano teachers. Teenagers are also welcome, accompanied by their teachers or their parents. Participants will have a one-hour lesson each day with Rami, a class, lecture, or concert performance each evening with Rami and guest masters, and at least four hours of daily piano time. You will learn correct and injury free piano playing techniques as well as many other aspects of piano playing.

http://rami.ybarniv.com/?page_id=198

PianoTexas International Academy & Festival, Young Artists Performers: up to 27 years old. No age limits for all other programs. Fort Worth, Texas. Sections for Young Artists Performers, Young Artists Active, General Observers, and Teacher/Amateurs.

PianoTexas International Academy & Festival seeks to provide a high-level educational opportunity for outstanding pre-college and college piano students, piano teachers, and adult amateurs from all over the world through public performances and interaction with renowned performing artists, instructors and other music professionals. www.pianotexas.org

The Alan Fraser Piano Institute, ages 9 and up. Locations in Cleveland Ohio, Holland Michigan, Amherst Massachusetts, Concord New Hampshire, Ogden Utah, and Split Croatia. Alan Fraser has written four books linking Feldenkrais Method to piano technique. He teaches "skeletal" piano playing, synthesizing the best of the finger action, arm weight and rotation schools. Students report breakthroughs in their sound, their ability to phrase with feeling, their sense of agility, and their ability to learn music quickly. This approach also effectively addresses performance injury issues. The institute accepts pianists of all levels: concert artists, studio teachers, students and amateurs. Each day includes a Feldenkrais Awareness Through Movement lesson, individual piano lessons (observed by all unless otherwise requested), and a lecture on aspects of technique such as the hand's arches, the thumb, rotation, arm weight, octaves and chords, elasticity, phrasing and rhythmic inflection. The Alan Fraser Piano Institute will take your playing and teaching to the next level on the fine Steinway pianos of Cleveland State University, the University of Massachusetts, Browning Arts Center at Weber State University, Concord Community Music School, Anderson-Werkman Performing Arts Center of Hope College, and Split, Croatia.

http://www.pianotechnique.net/alanfraserinstitute/

Music Teachers National Association National Conference. The MTNA National Conference, held annually, brings together the most representative cross-section of the MTNA membership. National competitions feature the outstanding performances of students in all instrument areas, as well as composition. Conferences include master classes, technology and informational sessions, pedagogy sessions; exhibit hall, evening concerts, and much more. Members have an opportunity to participate by submitting proposals and papers for presentation.

In addition to these excellent national and international offerings, most states have music teachers' associations that hold annual or semiannual conferences with nationally known guest clinicians and concert artists. At these gatherings, attendees have the opportunity to witness masterclasses, take in lectures, and hear outstanding performances.

Maintaining, cultivating, and extending your skills as a pianist and teacher has dividends for you and your students. Although concrete advantages such as expanding your teaching toolbox and musical skill set are critical, perhaps the greatest advantage to continuing education is the feeling of motivation and self-renewal that occurs when teachers participate in lessons, workshops, and professional associations. Regularly tapping into this well of self-esteem is a necessary activity that all piano teachers should make a regular part of their professional life.

An annually updated listing of summer workshops can be found in *Clavier Companion* magazine, which is now available in print and online versions: https://www.claviercompanion.com

Professional Literature

Piano teachers who wish to consistently refine their craft should maintain subscriptions to the major journals in the fields of piano teaching and music education and should frequently read online forums for music teaching. While the content of these journals and forums varies from the highly scientific to the practical and applicable, all of the journals listed below offer excellent information from diverse perspectives:

Clavier Companion. This is the journal of the Frances Clark Center for Keyboard Pedagogy, which is available in both print and online versions. Articles feature informative, interesting, and inspiring ideas on all aspects of piano teaching and learning. https://claviercompanion.com

Piano Pedagogy Forum. The Piano Pedagogy Forum features content available online dating back to January 1998. It is available on the website of the Frances Clark Center for Keyboard Pedagogy, where it is available without a subscription. https://www.keyboardpedagogy.org/pianopedagogyforum

American Music Teacher. This is the print journal of the Music Teachers National Association. All members of MTNA receive AMT as a benefit of membership. Since 1951, *American Music Teacher* has provided articles, reviews and regular columns that inform, educate and challenge music teachers and foster excellence in the music teaching profession. Available online and in print. https://www.mtna.org/MTNA/Stay_Informed/American_Music_Teacher/American_Music_Teacher.aspx

MTNA e-Journal. The e-Journal is a peer-reviewed online-only journal from MTNA that features articles on all areas of the music teaching profession. Articles are in-depth, scholarly research-oriented articles that offer engaging and original perspectives. Articles typically feature audio and video examples: https://www.mtna.org/MTNA/Stay_Informed/MTNA_e-Journal/e-Journal_Submission_Information.aspx

Journals available from the National Association for Music Education. The association offers six periodicals, including *Music Educators Journal, Teaching Music, Journal of Research in Music Education, General Music Today, Update: Applications of Research in Music Education,* and *Journal of Music Teacher Education.* Some of these journals are available in print, and some are available online. Back issues are available. Further information can be found at https://nafme.org/my-classroom/journals-magazines/

International Journal of Music Education. Peer-reviewed journal published by the International Society for Music Education (ISME) four times a year. Manuscripts published are scholarly works, representing empirical research in a variety of modalities. Articles typically aim to enhance knowledge regarding the teaching and learning of music with a special interest toward an international constituency. http://journals.sagepub.com/home/ijm

Bulletin of the Council for Research in Music Education. Peer-reviewed journal that contains research and reviews of books of interest to the international music education profession. Published quarterly by the University of Illinois at Urbana-Champaign. http://bcrme.press.illinois.edu

Canadian Music Educator. This is the peer-reviewed journal of the Canadian Music Educators' Association. https://cmea.ca/journal/

Contributions to Music Education. The primary purpose of this journal is to recognize and highlight the importance of social science research in guiding educational practice. This is a peer-reviewed publication focused on issues related to music teaching and learning in school contexts. With over 40 years in print, CME has supported scholarly investigation into music education since 1972. http://www.omea-ohio.org/v3_resources/v3_resources/cme.html

Journal of Music Theory Pedagogy. The Journal of Music Theory Pedagogy is a project of the Gail Boyd de Stwolinski Center for Music Theory Pedagogy at the University of Oklahoma. The Center was established in 1985 to provide an international clearinghouse for information concerning the teaching and learning of music theory. https://music.appstate.edu/about/jmtp

Music Education Research. An international refereed journal with a focus on music education research as well as cross-cultural investigations and discussions relating to all areas of music education. http://www.tandfonline.com/loi/cmue20

Visions of Research in Music Education. A fully refereed critical journal appearing exclusively on the Internet. Its publication is offered as a public service to the profession by the New Jersey Music Educators Association, the state affiliate of NAfME. This journal is also associated with Westminster Choir College of Rider University in Princeton, New Jersey. http://www-usr.rider.edu/~vrme/

In addition to the scholarly journals listed above, music teaching blogs continue to appear online, providing a dynamic venue for consistently updated information. Some recommended blogs include the following.

The Piano Podcast with Mario Ajero: http://marioajero.blogspot.com

Tim Topham: https://timtopham.com

Music Matters Blog: http://musicmattersblog.com

Color in My Piano: http://colorinmypiano.com

Practising the Piano: http://www.practisingthepiano.com

Compose Create: https://composecreate.com

Teach Piano Today: https://www.teachpianotoday.com

Diane Hidy: http://dianehidy.com

This is by no means an exhaustive list of piano teaching resources online, not to mention the many forums available to piano teachers on social media that feature lively conversation and real-time interaction. The digital age has brought piano teachers a myriad of resources to help them stay informed and trained continuously.

INDEX

504 accommodations 180

ability grouping 12–13
abstract and application in students with high-functioning autism 72
academic code of conduct 148–9
academic integrity and the international student 148–9
accountability partners 144–5
active learning for undergraduates 102–6
ADHD co-morbidities 81–2
ADHD in adults 84
Adreon, Diane 68–9
adult learners by age group 34–5
Alan Fraser Piano Institute 209
alcohol use among undergraduates 90–1
American Music Teacher 34, 129, 211
American phrases, humor, idioms and slang and international students 146
anchor activities 15–16
Applied Behavior Analysis and Discrete Trail Training 69
appropriate teacher interventions for depression 61–3
Arrau, Claudio 158
assimilation 177
assisting non-native speakers of English 142–3
attributes of effective mentors 119

Attwood, Thomas 156–7
audiation 10

Bach, Carl Philipp Emanuel 152–4
background knowledge of international students 140–1
Barenboim, Daniel 158
Bauer, Beth 74–5
Beethoven, Ludwig van 96, 99–100, 102, 141, 143, 156–7, 165, 168, 202, 205
Beethoven's Buddies 74–5
Behaviorist Theory, Behaviorism 66
benefits of mentoring graduate students 120–2
best practices for mentors 124–5
bias 146–7
brain chemicals associated with learning 9
brain drain 138–9
Breithaupt, Rudolph 160
Briggs, Katharine Cook 181
Bruhn, Karl T. 37–9, 41–3
Bruhn's definition of Recreational Music Making 38
Brzuzua, Krysztof 1
Bulletin of the Council for Research in Music Education 212
burnout 41–5

Canadian Music Educator 212
Carolina LifeSong Initiative 74

INDEX

causes of depression 60–1
Celebrating the Spectrum: A Festival of Music and Life 75, 207
challenges faced by adult learners 24–6
characteristics of high-functioning autism 65–6
Chung, Brian 38–9
clarity of expectations in graduate student mentoring 124–5
classroom policies, assignments, and grading rubrics for international students 141–2
Clavier Companion 210
Clavinova 44–5, 50
Clementi, Muzio 152, 157
Color in My Piano 213
Columbia University 137
common knowledge 149
Compose Create 213
concept model 103
Conda, Michelle 34
consent and physical touch 110–11
continuing education for piano teachers 203–13
Contributions to Music Education 212
creating an effective emotional environment for gifted students 16–17
Cristofori, Bartolomeo 151–2
Czerny, Carl 157–9, 165, 171

Dawson, Geraldine 70
Deppe, Ludwig 160
depression and anxiety co-morbidity 6
depression rates 55–7
diagnosing ADHD 81–2
Dillon, Brenda 38–9
Dillon's definition of recreational music making 38
diverse piano personalities 181–9

effective learning environments for gifted students 15–16
emerging adulthood 34
emotional distress, anxiety and depression among graduate students 125
empty praise 100, 109

English proficiency requirements for international students 142–3
Essay on the True Art of Playing Keyboard Instruments 152–4
establishing a mentoring relationship 126–7
expectations in academia 123–4

Fay, Amy 159, 161, 172
Fischer, Edwin 158
Fleisher, Leon 165–7
flipped classroom 140
flow of international students 138–9
focal dystonia 166
focusing and maintaining concentration in a student with ADHD 83–7
Freystädtler, Franz Jakob 157
fulfilling dreams in Recreational Music Making 40

Gardner, Howard 186–8
Gardner's eight types of intelligence 186–8
General Music Today 211
gifted students in the piano studio 8–11
giftedness 6–8
goals and objectives for undergraduates 107–8
Gordon, Edwin E. 9–10

HealthRHYTHMS Group Empowerment Drumming 44
helping undergraduates develop critical thinking skills 100–2
Hidy, Diane 213
history of graduate education 117–18
history of Recreational Music Making 37–40
Howard Gardner's theory of multiple intelligences 186–8

imitating playful adults and high-functioning autism 73
imitative behaviors and high-functioning autism 72–4
impact of Recreational Music Making on beginning nursing students 41–3
imposter syndrome 130–1

216

INDEX

inclusion 177
individual education plan (IEP) 179–80
Individuals with Disabilities Act (IDEA) 178–9
initial meetings with graduate students 126–7
instruction for international students 139–47
instructional outlines for students with ADHD 85–6
International Journal of Music Education 212
international undergraduates 95–6
internationalization 135
IQ 6–8, 194

Johnsen and Ryser's five areas for differentiating instruction 13–15
Journal of Music Teacher Education 211
Journal of Music Theory Pedagogy 212
Journal of Research in Music Education 211
Juilliard School 3, 163–4
Jung, Carl 182
junior faculty expectations 129–30
Jutras, Peter 30

Kalkbrenner, Friedrich 160
Keirsey Temperament Sorter (KTS) 188–9
Kirby, Linda 67
Krause, Martin 158
Kullak, Theodor 158, 160

Landowska, Wanda 158
learner responsibility 112–15
learning goals 67, 94, 101, 106–7, 113–14
learning objectives 107, 114
leisure-benefit research and adult pianists 28–30
Leon Fleisher Archive at the Peabody Institute 167
Leschetizky, Theodor 158, 165
lesson and repertoire planning 112
LGBT students 132
Lhevinne, Josef 162–3
Lhevinne, Rosina 163–4
Lichnowsky, Karl 156
lifelong mentoring 129–31

Liszt, Franz 157–61, 171
Liszt's teaching style 159–62

maintaining a safe and professional relationship 110–12
majority-group discussion domination 133
merit-pay 125
Michigan State University 22, 75, 129, 136, 168, 203
Michigan State University College of Music Piano Retreat 203
minimizing stress and worry in a student with high-functioning autism 68–9
modeling effective use of time 123
modeling enthusiasm for academia 108–10
modeling professional integrity 124
models of evaluation for undergraduates 106–8
Moriarty, Deborah 75, 168, 207
Moscow Imperial Conservatory 163
Moszkowski, Moritz 158
motivation in adult pianists 23–4
Mozart, Wolfgang Amadeus 2, 14, 154–7, 165, 170, 171
Mozart's technique teaching 155–6
MTNA e-Journal 211
MTNA Recreational Music Making teaching track 48
multiculturalism 177
music aptitude 9–10
Music Education Research 212
Music Educators Journal 211
Music Matters Blog 213
Music Teachers National Association 48, 112, 123, 129, 209, 211
Music Teachers National Association National Conference 209
Myers-Briggs Type Indicator (MBTI) 181–6
Myers, Isabel Briggs 181

National Association of Music Merchants 38
National Center for Education Statistics criteria for nontraditional students 21–2

INDEX

National Conference on Keyboard Pedagogy (NCKP) 74, 129, 206–7
National Conference on Keyboard Pedagogy's committee for teaching students with special needs 74
National Piano Foundation Recreational Music Making teacher scholarship 48
National Research Center on the Gifted and Talented 7, 11
negative mood states 41
networking for junior faculty 130
New England Conservatory 168–9
number of adult learners 22–3

Ozonoff, Sally 70

pacing instruction for students with ADHD 85
Perkin's three strands of intelligence 7
Perkins, David 7
physical challenges in adult learners 24–5
physical comfort and accessibility in the teaching studio 111–12
piano andragogy 34
piano inventory worksheet 93–4
Piano Pedagogy Forum 211
piano teacher training 201–2
PianoTexas International Academy & Festival 208
Plagiarism 148
Ployer, Barbara 156
Pollack, Daniel 1–2, 105, 164
positive reinforcement 100–1
possible causes of ADHD 78–9
power dynamic 110–11
practical ideas for Recreational Music Making 49–51
Practising the Piano 213
Price, Scott 74, 207
Prokofiev, Sergei 158, 205
psychosocial pressures on adult learners 25–6

Rami's Rhapsody Piano Camp for Adults 208

Recreational Music Making
and coronary heart disease 46–7
and human stress response 46
and immunological responses in older adults 45–6
and long-term care workers 43–5
Recreational Music Making group teaching 40
Recreational Music Making performances 40
regular practice for the piano teacher 203–6
Rehabilitation Act of 1973 180
Renzulli, Joseph S. 7
Renzulli's "three-ring" description of giftedness 7–8
responsibilities of the mentor 122–4
role of graduate mentor 118–20
Romanowski Bashe, Pat 67
Rubinstein, Arthur 158
Russian tradition of piano teaching 162–4

Schnabel, Artur 164–5
Schuller, Gunther 169
Scope and Sequence 72
self-efficacy 101, 186
self-satisfaction 101
self-worth 3, 101, 114, 186
seven liberal arts of the ancient world 117
Sherman, Russell 168–70
Shevitz, Betty 71
show-off night 71
signs of depression 54–5
Simpson, Richard L. 72
simulation 104
Smith Myles, Brenda 72
social fragmentation 177
societal diversity in the piano studio 176–81
Socratic method 85, 98–9
stages of human development
  adolescence 191–6
  early childhood 189–91
Stella, Jennifer 68
Sternberg, Robert 6
Steuermann, Edward 168

INDEX

strategies for teaching adult pianists 26–30
strategies for undergraduate lectures 96–100
strategies for working with gifted students 13–15
student self-evaluation 114–15
subjects within piano pedagogy 202
sugar consumption and ADHD 79
suicide 57–60
suicide lethality assessment 58–9
supporting gifted females 17–19
supporting graduate students 128–9
syllabi for undergraduate courses 107–8
symptoms of ADHD 79–81

Taubman Piano Festival 207–8
TEACCH Method (Treatment and Education of Autistic and related Communication-handicapped Children program) 70
Teach Piano Today 213
teacher transitions for a student with high-functioning autism 68
Teaching Music 211
teaching strategies for students with high-functioning autism 67–9
teaching versus facilitating in Recreational Music Making 39
the benefits of piano study for adults 30–3
The Piano Podcast with Mario Ajero 213

three fields of graduate study in the ancient world 117–18
three main subcategories of ADHD 77–8
Topham, Tim 213
total mood disturbance 41–5
traditionally underrepresented students 132–3
training teachers of undergraduates 92–3
transition-planning meetings 68
treating ADHD 82–4
triarchic theory of intelligence 6

underrepresented gifted students 8
United States Census Bureau projections 176–7
University of Southern California 136, 164
Update: Applications of Research in Music Education 211

variables of burnout 41–5
Visions of Research in Music Education 213
Visual Learning, Auditory Learning, Read/Write Learning, Kinesthetic Learning Model (VAK/VARK) 188–9

Williams, Karen 68
Wings Mentor Program 71

Yamaha Corporation of America 37
Yesipova, Anna 158